THE
MOUNTAIN BIKE
BOOK

THE
MOUNTAIN BIKE
BOOK

DAVID LESLIE

PHOTOGRAPHS BY TIM WOODCOCK

WARD LOCK

A WARD LOCK BOOK

First published in the UK 1996
by Ward Lock
Wellington House
125 Strand
LONDON
WC2R 0BB

A Cassell Imprint
Volume Copyright © Ward Lock 1995, 1996
Text Copyright © David Leslie   1995, 1996

Distributed in the United States
by Sterling Publishing Co., Inc.
387 Park Avenue South, New York NY 10016-8810

A British Library Cataloguing in Publication Data block for this book may be obtained from the British Library

ISBN 0-7063-7524-6

Commissioning Editor: Stuart Cooper
Project Editor: Chris Catling
Consultant: Tim Woodcock
Designed and typeset by: Pardoe Blacker Publishing, Lingfield, Surrey
Illustrations by: Paul Weston

Printed and bound in Spain by Bookprint S.L.

CONTENTS

INTRODUCTION

Mountain biking is one of the fastest-growing outdoor activities, enjoyed by people of all ages and at all levels of attainment – for getting about on busy inner-city roads, or for the exciting sport of off-road biking. Mountain biking was just a novelty in the early 1980s, and yet now it has become an official Olympic sport.

Part of the appeal lies in the bicycles themselves: they are simply great fun to ride. To this is added the challenge of testing your mental and physical boundaries as you tackle a steep hillside trail or race along a forest path skilfully avoiding the obstacles.

Whatever your level of ability, few of us can claim to be an expert in all areas of mountain biking – there are just too many aspects to the sport. The aim of this book is to get you started and then point you in the right direction when it comes to making decisions. That way you will get more enjoyment from your riding and gain in confidence as you progress.

Maybe you have a bike already or are about to buy one. There are so many questions. Should I get this? Must it have one of those? What does this do? Where can I use this bike? How do I mend it? How do I get fit?

I will answer these questions by taking you through all the elements of mountain bikes: how they are built and put together, the components and how they work, and how to service and repair things when they go wrong.

Cycling has also spawned its own distinctive style in clothing – designed to look good and give protection against the elements while remaining sleekly aerodynamic! I will take you through the clothing and what it is supposed to do. I will explain why cycle clothing is different from other outdoor clothing and, more importantly, point out what to look for when you buy.

Mountain biking can be a very demanding sport physically. I will show you how to get more enjoyment out of your riding by getting fitter and eating the right foods.

Most of us have a dream that involves travel, and having a bike will help you on your way. Sections on how to travel with your bike will guide you through the range of transport options. There is advice on riding in various countries to whet your appetite and practical tips for planning a cycling holiday.

Whether you are a beginner or an experienced cyclist, look upon this book as a constant companion, a source of help when you need information or reassurance, and a guide to getting the best out of your mountain bike, wherever in the world you choose to ride.

(LEFT) The call of the wild: the thrill of mountain biking comes from reaching places where ordinary bikes cannot go.

THE MOUNTAIN BIKE

What is a mountain bike and what makes it different from ordinary cycles? This section takes a comprehensive look at mountain bikes, their structure and their components. It will give you the knowledge you need to make informed decisions when buying your bike. It will also tell you how all the bits work, and how to service, repair or replace components so as to keep your bike in tip-top condition.

The Frame

The materials used to make a bike frame today vary enormously, though the only visible difference may be in the price tag. Working on the basis that the more a bike costs the better it must be is not always a wise assumption. A good frame may come with poorer-quality components, or vice versa. Making direct price comparisons is only a very rough guide – far better is to understand the various materials available and the techniques used to join the parts of the frame together.

Saddle

Seat post

Rear light

Cable stop

Seat post
quick release

Rear
reflector

Seat tube

Air
pump

Rear brake

Front
derailleur
mechanism

Seat stay

Sprocket cluster
and freewheel

Rear wheel

Wheel nuts

Gear cable

Crank
arm

SPD
pedal

Rear derailleur
mechanism

Bottom bracket

Chain stay

Chain

Chain rings

A TYPICAL MOUNTAIN BIKE

Front light

Gear shifter

Brake lever

Top tube

Handlebar stem

Headset

Brake cable

Head tube

Front reflector

Water bottle

Front brake

Front wheel

Valve

Spoke

Tyre

Down tube

Forks

Hub

Rim

The most common materials used in bike frame construction are steel, chrome molybdenum (a steel alloy), aluminium, titanium and carbonfibre.

Mountain bike frames

Steel: strong and reliable, steel is cheap to manufacture and easy to work with. Its great deficiency, from the mountain bike point of view, is its weight. The very best (and most expensive) steel frames are made from alloys (that is, mixtures of steel with other metals) such as chrome molybdenum, which is lighter than steel but just as strong.

Aluminium: though lighter than steel, aluminium requires thicker tube sections to achieve the same strength. This reduces the aerodynamic properties of the bike, but not to any noticeable degree. The cheaper aluminium frames lack flexibility, resulting in a hard ride, but the best aluminium frames are up to 20 per cent lighter than steel.

Titanium: light, strong and flexible, titanium frames are also the most expensive because the metal itself is difficult to extract from its ore and difficult to work. The high cost may be off-putting, but titanium frames are long-lasting, resistant to fatigue and they give a softer ride.

Carbonfibre: this material is very light and strong and it is cheaper than titanium, comparing in price with the best steel or aluminium frames. Although the strength-to-weight ratio is good, carbonfibre is liable to impact fatigue – a heavy impact will weaken its structure and can lead to what is called 'poor second impact strength'. This means that a second impact, even of low force, can result in dramatic frame failure.

Choosing your frame

Choosing a frame will always be a compromise between lightness, strength, flexibility, longevity and expense. Lightweight frames give better bike handling: unfortunately the lighter materials are often more expensive. For your first-ever bike, chrome molybdenum (or

'chromoly') end bracket frames probably represent the best option, but do look carefully at the specifications and ensure that the whole frame is made of chromoly; chain stays, seat stays and forks can be of ordinary steel.

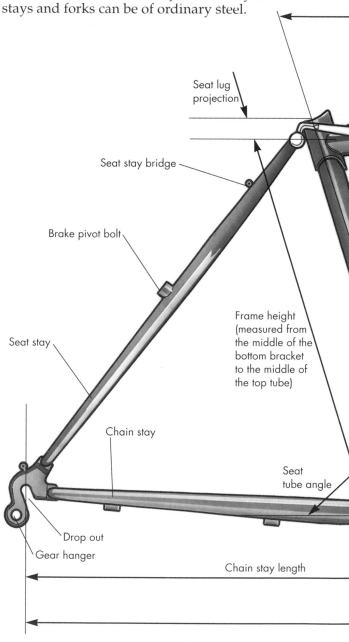

Seat lug projection

Seat stay bridge

Brake pivot bolt

Seat stay

Chain stay

Frame height (measured from the middle of the bottom bracket to the middle of the top tube)

Seat tube angle

Drop out

Gear hanger

Chain stay length

Frame size is measured from the bottom bracket to either the top of the seat tube, the top tube, or the seat cluster, depending on the manufacturer.

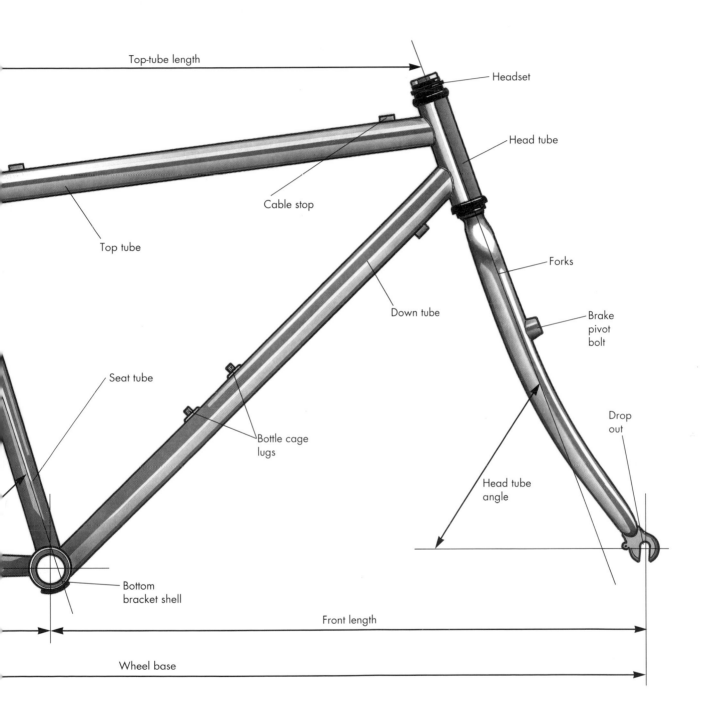

Top-tube length

Headset

Head tube

Cable stop

Top tube

Forks

Down tube

Brake
pivot
bolt

Seat tube

Drop
out

Bottle cage
lugs

Head tube
angle

Bottom
bracket shell

Front length

Wheel base

A MOUNTAIN BIKE FRAME

Joining techniques

The way frames are joined together affects their weight and strength. Several technical terms are used to describe these joining techniques. Here is an explanation of what they mean.

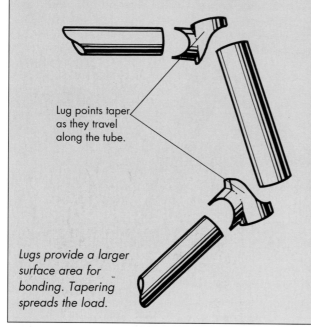

Lug points taper as they travel along the tube.

Lugs provide a larger surface area for bonding. Tapering spreads the load.

Butting or double butting: this term is used to describe tubes with thickened walls at the joints. Thinner walls save weight but thicker walls provide stronger joints.

TIG welded steel: Tungsten inert gas (TIG) welding is commonly used to fuse together sections of tubing. This does away with the need for lugs, further reducing weight.

TIG welded aluminium: a variation on this technique involves the grinding smooth of the telltale feathering left after the point has been welded. This results in a smoother curved weld that spreads the load better.

Bonded aluminium: the joints are glued together to avoid heat damage to the aluminium. This is a very strong fixing method.

Aluminium lugs: since carbonfibre cannot be welded, aluminium lugs are used instead. These form a sleeve that fits over two or more parts. Lugs are usually bonded with epoxy resin.

Lugless fillet brazing: when a custom frame is being built at odd angles lugs cannot be used so a build-up of brazing is employed instead.

Frame shapes

The majority of mountain-bike frames conform to the traditional design of a double triangle within a diamond. Other designs have been tried but none gives the same rigidity, strength or handling characteristics. Bikes with some kind of suspension system (as opposed to a rigid frame) often break away from the traditional concept, but at a much higher cost. Even within the traditional shape, there is scope for varying the geometry of the frame so as to alter the comfort, handling, acceleration and stability of the bike. These are the major variables.

Chain stays: the chain stay is the part of the frame that runs from the pedals to the back wheel. Short stays aid acceleration and hill-climbing. Longer stays are more stable and provide for better load positioning. When climbing, the centre of gravity needs to be over the rear wheel to provide maximum grip. Short stays help achieve this. Tall people will have their centre of gravity closer to the contact point because the longer seat post will be pushed further back by the seat post angle.

Top tube: this is the horizontal tube that runs from the handlebar stem to the seat post. In mountain bikes, this often slopes down from front to rear. A sloping top tube provides more torsional and lateral stiffness. The length of the top tube is important for handlebar reach. If you are too stretched out, your arms and hands will suffer. If you are too upright, there will be too much weight on the back of the bike, and climbing will be more difficult.

Head tube: this short tube runs from the handlebars to the front forks. It houses the front-wheel steerer. A longer head tube is used by some manufacturers to provide more support for the headset bearings. Lengthening the headtube adds to the slope of top tubes.

TOURING BIKES

If you are buying a bike to use on extended tours and for carrying panniers there are a few additional points to consider when choosing the frame. Does it have lugs for carriers or can they be fitted? This may be a problem on carbonfibre frames. Larger frames offer more stability when carrying loads. Longer chain stays will provide better clearance for the panniers and a more comfortable ride.

Clearance: *allow standover clearance of 3 to 4 inches between your crotch and the frame.*
Seat post: *should be 6 to 8 inches or more for mountain bikes.*
Seat position: *determined by the length of the thigh.*

For mountain biking, it is recommended that you use the smallest frame that is comfortable. Small frames are lighter and more flexible. Good bike shops will take great trouble to ensure that you choose the right sized frame, using an adjustable fitting machine.

Handlebar height: *should be at, or just below, the level of the saddle.*
Handlebar width: *should be the same as the width of your shoulders, plus the width of your hands.*
Saddles: *for women, should be wider to support the pelvic girdle.*
Pedal position: *the ball of your foot should be over the pedal axle.*

Relative to their height, women have shorter torsos and arms than men. To compensate, it is best to increase the seat post height and angle, and reduce the frame size. The ideal size is one that allows the back to be straight and the arms slightly bent to absorb shocks.

Down tube: this tube runs from the head tube down to the bottom bracket to absorb pressure from the front fork. Manufacturers have experimented with removing this tube and replacing it with a wire, though this weight-saving idea puts extra strain on the top tube.

Bottom bracket: this houses the pedal bearing. The higher it is, the greater the ground clearance of the pedals and chainrings. The lower it is, the lower the bike's centre of gravity.

Wheelbase: bikes with short wheelbases are more agile, but bikes with longer wheelbases are more comfortable to ride.

Flex and stiffness

A bike's flexibility depends on the materials from which the frame is made. Materials such as aluminium and carbonfibre are more flexible than steel. The more the frame flexes the more comfortable it is over rough ground. The stiffer the frame the more efficient the transfer of peddling to forward motion. There is obviously a point of compromise between the two.

Flexing occurs in all bike parts, some of which do not effect comfort. By reducing the flex from the drive-train components, the frame can be allowed a little more flexibility.

Sizing a bike

Men and women have different shapes and this will affect your choice. Generally women have longer legs and a shorter torso and arms than men of the same height. This means that women need a bike with a shorter top tube, a longer and steeper seat tube and a shorter stem than a man of the same height. Having made these adjustments, it may be necessary to alter the length of the pedal cranks – the pedal cranks should be shorter for short-legged people.

Try a variety of different makes, since they all differ in small ways. Brand loyalty is a condition spread by clever marketing. Do not let it interfere with your basic aim – to get a properly fitting bike.

The first time that you get on a mountain bike, you may find that the correct position and size may feel alien and even uncomfortable. One common mistake is to choose a frame that is too big. Men and women both need plenty of so-called 'standover' – the distance between the top tube and the crutch. This is because you will often need to leap off the saddle and place your feet on the ground

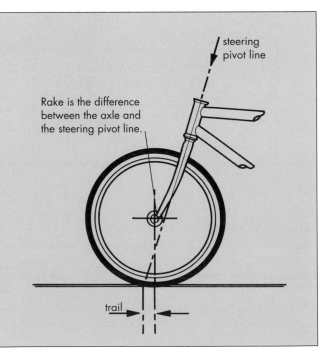

TRAIL

If you draw a line down the head tube to the ground it will pass behind the front-wheel axle. The spot where the line reaches the ground is the pivot point. If you draw another line from the axle down to the ground this will fall behind the pivot point. The distance between these two points is measured as trail. The offset of the pivot line from the axle is known as rake. Change the rake or the head-tube angle and you change the trail.

As trail is increased the steering becomes heavier and less responsive, but humps and bumps will not shake the front wheel around so much. If your mountain bike had no trail at all the steering would feel very 'twitchy' – in other words, the front wheel would buck and twist every time it hit a stone or bump.

steering pivot line

Rake is the difference between the axle and the steering pivot line.

trail

as you negotiate rough tracks and steep gradients. Allowing plenty of standover clearance will avoid discomfort or even serious injury. The seat should stand at least six or more inches (15 cm) above the top tube.

The bike may feel small compared with ordinary bikes, but you will soon get used to the feel.

Now that you have some idea of the materials from which bike frames are made, and how they are put together, you can consider choosing a bike. Think about how much you can afford to spend and set yourself a budget. Within that budget, you need to consider whether to go for a more expensive frame with lower-grade components, or a lower-grade frame with better components .

Sizing points

● Adjust the saddle position so that your leg is straight, but not stretched, when it is at the bottom of the pedal stroke. Make sure that the seat post is not extended beyond its limit, or it will snap.

● The combined length of the top tube and handlebar stem should provide for a riding position where your arms are slightly relaxed and able to absorb shock. You should not feel stretched out or too upright. If the rest of the bike fits then experiment with handlebar stems of different lengths and rise.

Components

The components fitted to a bike frame are what make it function. The range of components is huge, and your head will soon be in a spin as you try to weigh up the pros and cons of each. Even so, it is necessary to try and understand as much as you can about them and avoid being taken in by the marketing hype of bike manufacturers, who do their best to convince you that their range is the best available.

When looking at components you must consider factors such as price, weight, use, servicing needs and durability. How cool it looks on your machine, whether the colour matches your eyes, and whether the brand name is hip should only be used to help you choose between two otherwise equal products as a final consideration.

Wheels

Mountain-bike wheels are traditionally measured in inches. This is rather odd for such a new sport: it would have made more sense to use metric measurements. Standard wheels have a 26-inch diameter, though 24-inch diameter wheels are available. Unless you are a child or a small adult, it is best to stick to 26-inch wheels. The market for 24-inch wheels (and inner tubes) is limited and this is reflected in their availability.

Despite its fragile appearance, a bicycle wheel is extremely strong. As well as supporting the weight of the bike and rider, wheels also transfer peddled and steering energy through them. How well they achieve this is partly a factor of the design, partly of the component materials and partly of the way they are made.

We know why wheels need to be strong, but why are they so flimsy? One of the biggest considerations in bike design is weight. This is even more important in wheel design. The lighter a wheel, the less energy is required to turn it. Road-bike racers have a maxim that says: 'an ounce off the wheel is worth a pound off the frame'. This rather exaggerated saying is true enough in principal. A pound of weight on the wheel requires a great deal more energy to propel the bike than a pound on the frame.

A lot of the energy expended in accelerating a bike is used to build up the spinning speed of all the rotating parts. The further the weight is away from the axis of a spinning object the more energy is required to turn it.

HOW DOES A WHEEL WORK?

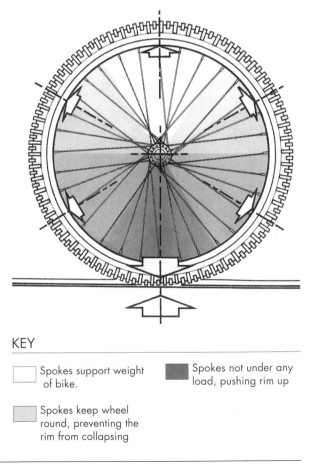

KEY

☐ Spokes support weight of bike.

☐ Spokes keep wheel round, preventing the rim from collapsing

■ Spokes not under any load, pushing rim up

While this effect applies to some extent to chainrings, its consequences for a 26-inch wheel are much greater. It follows that saving weight on the rims, tyres and tubes will have more benefit than saving the same weight on the hub. Equally it is essential to keep the wheels clean of mud, otherwise you will lose all the benefits of lightweight wheels.

Rims

Wheel rims are usually made from steel or aluminium alloy. Aluminium is lighter and the surface offers greater friction, resulting in improved braking. Aluminium-alloy wheels are formed using box sections. Braking causes wear on the wheel rims, making them thinner. Eventually they become too thin and split. Some rims are reinforced by the application of a ceramic layer. Such rims are costly but they last longer and give improved braking.

Eyelets made of brass or steel are used to reinforce the area where the spoke nipples are seated. Reinforced in this way the rim weight can be shaved a little more, which helps to counteract the extra weight of the eyelets. Some rims come with double eyelets. These share the load between the two walls of the box section that the spoke nipple sits in.

Anodising

Aluminium alloy reacts with the air to become pitted and covered in oxide. This should not impair its performance but it does look scruffy. The electrolite process of anodising prevents this by giving the aluminium a thin protective coating. The use of different compounds in the process can also be used to change the colour.

This treatment does not increase the strength of the aluminium. Anodising was originally reserved as a process for coating superior alloys. This led some people to believe that it was a mark of quality or strength. Now it is used simply to make things looks pretty.

Spokes and nipples

Where the spoke passes through the wheel rim, the area surrounding it takes the load. The smaller the number of spokes in a wheel,

Exotic wheels

Instead of having spokes, the Tioga disc wheel is laced together using a fibre called Kevlar, which is then covered with a stick-on sheet to protect the strands. The result is a light wheel with a softer ride, but with the disadvantage that disc wheels are affected by cross winds.

the greater the load around each spoke cyelet and the stronger the rim needs to be. Stronger rims mean more weight, which we don't want, but more spokes also mean more weight, so wheel designers look for the optimum balance between the two. Ordinary bikes have 36 spokes but mountain bikes have stronger rims to absorb heavy impact loads from the ground. This allows the number of spokes to be reduced to 32.

The wide tyres used on mountain bikes provide a bigger surface area for grip, but they also help to spread impact loads along the rim. The higher the tyre pressure the greater the spread. Tyres like this allow the rim to be even lighter, so there is still plenty of strength in 32-spoke wheels to accommodate lighter rims. Even so, 36-spoke wheels have their uses: their extra strength is ideal for tandems or heavily laden touring bikes.

Stainless steel spokes are easy to clean, do not rust and last for ages. Titanium, carbonfibre and Kevlar are other alternatives but, unless you have very specialist needs and a fat wallet, they are not worth considering. Chrome-plated steel spokes, which do rust, are too brittle for a mountain bike. Galvanised steel spokes will corrode and seize any type of nipple.

Spokes are normally 14 gauge in thickness. If they were made any thinner they would be liable to fail at the thread. The commonest failure point is, in fact, at the elbow or bend, where the spokes join the hub. Failure in the middle of the spoke is rare, so spokes have been developed that are thinner in the middle section (16 gauge), and thicker (14 gauge) at the ends.

TOOLS FOR BIKE REPAIR AND MAINTENANCE

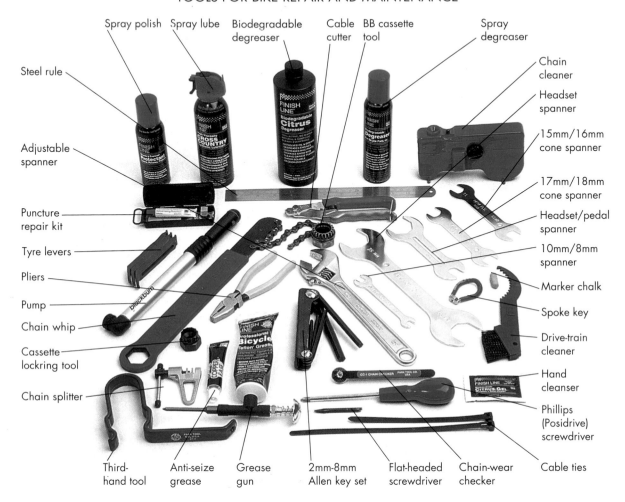

Spray polish · Spray lube · Biodegradable degreaser · Cable cutter · BB cassette tool · Spray degreaser

Steel rule

Adjustable spanner

Puncture repair kit

Tyre levers

Pliers

Pump

Chain whip

Cassette lockring tool

Chain splitter

Chain cleaner · Headset spanner · 15mm/16mm cone spanner · 17mm/18mm cone spanner · Headset/pedal spanner · 10mm/8mm spanner · Marker chalk · Spoke key · Drive-train cleaner · Hand cleanser · Phillips (Posidrive) screwdriver

Third-hand tool · Anti-seize grease · Grease gun · 2mm-8mm Allen key set · Flat-headed screwdriver · Chain-wear checker · Cable ties

Nipples serve two functions. They are used for fixing the spokes to the rim and adjusting and tensioning the spokes. In the interests of weight saving, aluminium alloy nipples are often used, but these can cause galvanic corrosion when used with steel spokes. Lubrication is the best defence. Try spraying the nipples with penetrating oil and tweaking them with a spoke key occasionally, but never tweak them more than a quarter of a turn one way and then a quarter of a turn back, otherwise that carefully stressed and balanced wheel will look like a taco shell.

Better still, use brass nipples, which are only slightly heavier, but do not corrode and are also a lot easier to adjust.

Wheel truing

Wheels have a tendency to deform from their ideal straight alignment and circular shape. This is quite natural, and small deformations are no cause for concern, but you must not let the wheel get too far out of shape. Usually the first signs you will notice are when the brake pads start to rub at one spot on the rim.

Before you set about truing a wheel, check to see if the axle is bent or whether there is too much play in the bearings. Both of these faults can make the wheel wobble and catch the brake blocks.

The wheel can be trued in a purpose-designed stand or left in the bike frame. In

Wheel truing

Tools: spoke key (make sure it is the correct size). Chalk to mark deviations.

Parts: spokes to replace those that are broken or badly damaged.

1. To check for concentric inaccuracies, spin the wheel and look for any low or raised sections. Mark both ends of the 'low' section. Loosen the spokes a quarter of a turn anti-clockwise along that section. Tighten the other spokes evenly until the 'low' section is pushed out. With 'raised' sections tighten the spokes to pull the rim in and slacken off the other spokes.

3. Check the dishing of the wheel (the concave shape) to ensure it is even on both sides of the hub. Measure the distance from each side of the wheel to the fork or the chainstay. If the wheel is off centre, tighten the nipples on the side with the widest gap by a quarter of a turn. If the gap on the rear-wheel drive side is the widest, only give the nipples an eighth of a turn. If this doesn't true the wheel loosen the nipples on the narrower side by an equivalent amount before repeating the process.

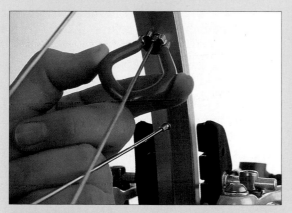

2. The position of any side-to-side imperfections should again be marked on the rim. Slacken off the spokes on the 'bulging' side by a quarter of a turn and tighten the spokes on the other side by the same amount. If the rim goes too far in the other direction, then ever so slightly retighten the spokes you slackened off first.

4. Finally, place the wheel on its side on the floor. Place your hands on the rim and press down. Repeat this at 6inch (15cm) intervals around the wheel. This will bed the rim in – you will hear the wheel pinging. Now check the wheel once more to make sure that the bedding in hasn't released any more imperfections.

Spoke key

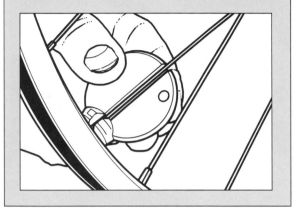

Use a good-quality spoke key that fits the nipples snugly. This is especially important with soft alloy nipples, which will deform and become impossible to turn if you use the wrong size of key.

either case, remove the tyre, tube and rim tape. If these are left on the wheel, the high inflation pressure of the tyre on the wheel rim will affect your truing attempts.

If you are replacing a spoke, do not bend it until it is through the hub flange. Fit the nipple after lightly oiling the spoke thread, then screw the nipple until it is lightly tensioned.

Wheel lacing

Building a wheel is one job you should leave to the expert. Get it wrong and you will cause a lot of expensive damage.

Even so, it is worth understanding why spokes are built the way they are. Spokes leave the hub flange at an acute angle, and they weave (or lace) over the next spoke, and under the next, before joining the rim. This pattern holds the rim stable, whereas a simple radial pattern of spokes would result in the hub twisting backwards and forwards under pedalling, quickly leading to a buckled wheel.

It is commonly believed that tight spokes make the wheel stronger and support the rim better. In fact, the real reason for high spoke tension has to do with fatigue life. Steel spokes have a stress life that is determined by the number of times they are stressed and relaxed. If the spokes are prestressed, it follows that an even greater stress is required to make a significant impact on the spokes.

Tyres

One of the most distinctive features of a mountain bike is its tyres. Big thick knobbly tyres define a mountain bike for some people. Obviously such tyres are needed to provide grip. How well a tyre performs this function will vary according to the surface conditions, tread pattern and tyre pressure.

For thick glutinous mud, tread patterns tend to be ribbed, with well-spaced block patterns. The more acutely angled, and the more closely together these small blocks of tread are placed, the more comfortable the ride and the better the grip on hard surfaces. The large stick-out pattern on the edge of some tyres is there to help the wheel climb up the side of ruts and to help it hold onto the sides of steep slopes. You'll notice that the blocks almost join in the centre on some tyres. This forms an almost continuous contact area for improved performance on solid surfaces.

Tyres are available in other colours than black. Grey, green or red are just some of the choices available. The colour differences are

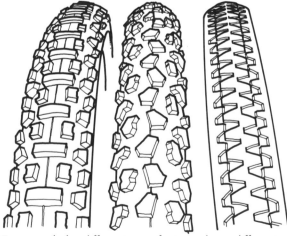

Tyres made by different manufacturers have different tread patterns, but all are wide and thick, with a deep tread to provide extra grip in difficult conditions.

Tyre width and pressure

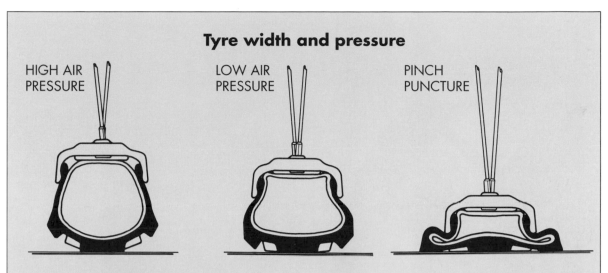

HIGH AIR PRESSURE

LOW AIR PRESSURE

PINCH PUNCTURE

• Whether to use thick or thin tyres depends on the terrain you intend to ride over. Thin tyres cut through mud better. Thick wide tyres, however, are more comfortable over rough services.

• Tyre pressures should be set high enough to avoid pinch punctures (which occur when some object traps the inner tube against the wheel rim) but low enough to allow the tyre to flex and then dislodge mud from between the tread pattern. Within these limits it is possible to vary the pressure slightly according to the riding conditions. Lower pressure puts a larger surface area of the tyre in contact with the ground, giving more grip. Higher tyre pressures cut down on pinch punctures. Higher pressures also put less tyre in contact with the ground, thus decreasing rolling resistance.

not devised for fashion-conscious bikers, but indicate the use of special compounds, designed to improve grip. Unfortunately, these special tyres do not wear very well.

Because the front and rear tyres perform different functions (one drives and the other steers) it makes sense that tread patterns should be different. Some tyres have the same tread pattern but simply point in opposite directions. Others have specific patterns designed especially for front or rear-wheel use.

Replacing a tyre

Running around both edges of a tyre wall is a bead, normally enclosing a steel wire, but sometimes made of Kevlar (see *Kevlar confusion*). The bead is smaller in diameter than the outside of the wheel rim: that is why it is sometimes difficult to get the tyre over the rim.

One way to make the task easier is to push the tyre into the well, or trough, that lies just inside the rim (ie do not push the tyre rim too far down inside the wheel). Seating the tyre beading in the trough of the rim provides just enough slack to enable the tyre to be slid snugly over the rim. When the tyre is inflated, the beading will be pushed up against the inside of the rim wall and out of the trough, but because the bead has a smaller diameter than the wheel, it cannot ride back over the rim.

Kevlar confusion

Tyres made from the proprietary compound called Kevlar are credited with three main benefits: lightness, foldability and puncture resistance. Tyres with Kevlar beading are around 1½ ounces (40g) lighter and more flexible because they do not have the steel beading that is used to reinforce the rims of ordinary tyres. Only tyres with Kevlar in the side walls can be claimed as puncture resistant. If you buy Kevlar tyres for puncture resistance make sure they are not just Kevlar beaded.

Tube replacement and puncture repair

Tools: tyre levers. Spanners for wheel removal if QRs not fitted. Pump.

Parts: inner tube and puncture kit.

1. Remove the wheel and clean off any excess mud from the wheel and tyre. Make sure the tube is fully deflated.

Ease the tyre over the wheel rim. Sometimes you can do this by hand, but you should avoid pinching the tube against the rim. Often it is easier to use a tyre lever to lift the tyre above the rim. Place another lever next to the first under the tyre, being careful not to pinch the tube, and slide it around the rim, prising the tyre over the rim as you do so.

Check the inside of the tyre for puncture-causing objects before fitting a new tube. Be careful when you do this: you don't want to injure yourself on a sharp object, such as a thorn or a piece of glass.

2. When you replace the inner tube, start by fitting the valve through the rim and screwing on the valve cap. It helps to keep the tube in place if you put a bit of air in it before you feed the tube inside the tyre.

Now put the tyre back inside the wheel rim. As the tension increases on the tyre make sure that the inner tube is not trapped between the rim and the tyre. To get the final bit of beading over the rim, seat the tyre in the trough of the rim on the opposite side of the wheel. Before inflating the inner tube make sure it isn't trapped at any point between the tyre and the rim.

Puncture repairs: When you do repair the puncture, make sure that the inner tube is clean and dry. Inflate the tube, and if the hole isn't obvious, feel around for the escaping air. If you can't find it using your hand, place the tube close to your lips and turn it until you can feel the escaping air. When you have located one hole always check to see if there are any more.

Roughen the tube surface slightly to allow the glue to key to the surface better. Mark the puncture(s) and deflate the tube. Apply glue to the tube and wait for it to go tacky – you will see the glue lose its shine.

Apply a chamfered patch to the puncture (chamfered, or feathered, patches are far better than normal patches). Now leave the repair to set (if you are putting the tube straight back in the tyre use the French chalk supplied to prevent the excess glue bonding the tube to the inside of the tyre).

Once the inner tube is returned to the tyre and inflated, check schrader-type valves for leaks by putting some saliva on your finger and placing it over the valve; if it bubbles, the valve is leaking. Depress the valve needle and the blast of air will normally clear the problem. When it is extremely cold, ice crystals can form and become lodged in the valve during inflation, preventing the valve from sealing – again, a blast of air is often sufficient to clear this.

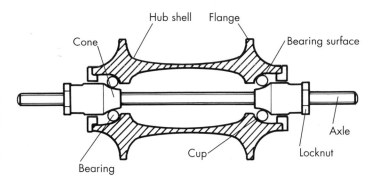

FRONT CUP-AND-CONE HUB

Some tyres have rims that bend inwards to form a hooked-bead rim. The hook traps the tyre more securely against the rim, allowing higher tyre pressures to be used. Greater care is needed when inflating the innertube with a hooked rim, to avoid trapping it between the tyre and the rim. On the other hand, tyres on hooked rims can be removed more easily by hand, without the need for tyre levers.

Inner tubes and valves

It is possible to buy inner tubes made from compounds (such as butyl or latex) that make them more resistant to punctures, though these are more expensive than ordinary tubes. Valves on inner tubes come as either presta (press on) or schrader fit (screw on car type).

Hubs

Hubs sit at the centre of the wheel and they contain the bearings around which the wheel turns.

The design of the front-wheel hub is very simple. It consists of a hollow tube with a cup at each end to support the axle bearings. There are also flanges at each end to house the spokes that support the wheel.

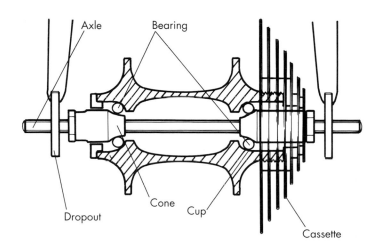

FREEHUB

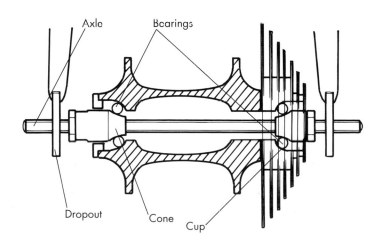

FREEWHEEL ON NORMAL HUB

Servicing the hub bearings

1. Take the wheel off the bike and remove the quick-release nut. To remove the sprocket set from the back wheel, wrap a chain whip round the second largest sprocket so that it pulls the sprocket set in a clockwise direction. Fit the lockring-removal tool over the lockring. To help hold the lockring-removal tool in place, put the quick-release nut back on and screw it up gently. Place an adjustable spanner over the lockring-removal tool and turn it anticlockwise, using the chain whip to pull the sprocket set in the opposite direction, and then loosen the lockring. Remove the quick-release nut, the lockring-removal tool, the lockring and the sprocket set, with its spacers or washer, remembering the order in which they should be returned.

3. If your hub has dust caps, these can be gently peeled aside. Now you can remove the bearings. Inspect and replace any cones and bearings that show signs of rust, wear or pitting. Look out, too, for dents and ripple-like indentations caused by the stress of repeated impacts on loose cones. Bearings that are to be reused should be kept in their sets. Make sure that bearings go back with the same cones and cups from which they came. Normally, though, old bearings should be replaced with new ones.

2. On the other side of the wheel, loosen the locknut from the cone. Remove the locknut and any spacers, remembering their position. As you pull the axle from the hub, keep it horizontal over a container (such as a basin) so that you don't lose any bearings. To remove the freehub, place a 10mm Allen key into the freehub body and turn it anticlockwise to remove the retaining bolt.

4. Thoroughly clean all the parts and surfaces with degreaser. Put new grease in the cups and place the bearings in the grease. Refit the dustcaps by pushing them in gently; if more force is required, then tapping with a soft rubber surface should do. If you have to resort to wood, be sure not to leave splinters behind.

Tools: spanners for wheel removal if QRs not fitted. Cone spanners for adjusting cones. Container for catching and holding bearings. Chain whip, cassette lockring tool and adjustable spanner for rear cassette removal.

Parts: bearings and grease. Cones if old ones pitted. If hubs pitted they may need replacing.

5. Assemble the drive-side axle first, replacing the cone and locknut, together with any spacers. Screw the locknut tight up to the cone ensuring that ³⁄₁₆in (5mm) of axle sticks out. Refit any seals. Push the axle through the hub so that the cone is pressed against the bearings. Check that you have not lost any bearings from the other cup. Refit the cones, spacers and locknut in the same order that they were removed.

6. Tighten the cone until it binds against the bearings. Slacken it off slightly so that the wheel rotates freely. Tighten the locknut up to the cone. If you've got it right, there will be the tiniest bit of play. This small bit of movement will be removed when the wheel is clamped back in the frame.

The rear hub is more complex, because it has to enable the wheel to turn freely in one direction (ie freewheel), but lock in the other direction so that power can be transferred from the pedals, via the chain and back-wheel sprockets, to the wheel, thus making the bicycle move.

To allow the wheel to turn freely in one direction, a freewheel mechanism is used, and there are two main types – the most modern of these is the so-called 'freehub' (sometimes known as a cassette freewheel) and the more traditional version is the screw-on freewheel (sometimes known as a freewheel block).

Most mountain bikes are fitted with the freehub design, which was developed by the Shimano company. Other hub manufacturers have now adopted this design, but not all systems are compatible – Campagnolo components, for example, will not necessarily fit all freehub types.

Freehubs can vary in several other ways. Some are forged to form a single piece of alloy. Others use alloy which is machined rather than forged. Some have separate components for the flanges and the centre tubes. The centre tubes themselves can be made from light-

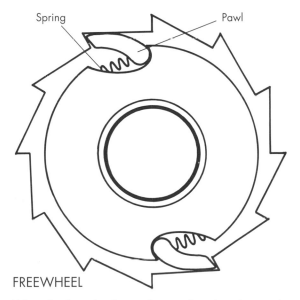

FREEWHEEL

When the freewheel turns in one direction, the pawls drive the hub body. When there is no drive, the pawls are pushed down by the ratchet in the hub body.

Grease nipples

Some hubs have grease nipples fitted, usually in the hub casing. These allow lubricant to be squeezed in behind the bearings, pushing out water and muck with the old grease. It is possible to drill a hub and insert your own nipple, but this may weaken the hub.

weight titanium, carbonfibre or alloy and then screwed or glued to a strong alloy flange. Hubs constructed in this way normally use sealed cartridge bearings.

Quick releases

Quick release systems (QRs) were developed to allow wheels to be removed and fitted quickly and without tools. QRs have hollow axles rather than more conventional solid ones. A threaded skewer passes through the hollow axles, with a cam device at one end and an adjuster at the other. When the cam is turned it pulls the adjuster tight, placing the skewer under tension.

Upgrading your QR from steel is a popular weight saver, but if you can live without the anodised colours that seem to motivate most QR upgrades, there are better ways to spend your money.

The big downside of a QR is the ease with which a thief can steal your wheel.

Quick release systems have levers that allow the wheel to be released or locked to the frame in seconds, without additional tools.

Bearings, cones and cups

All the weight and movement of a bicycle has to be handled by the bearings. They are thus vital components but they are often neglected because they are out of sight. The bearings themselves can be replaced if they become worn, but the cups in which they sit are part of the hub, and once these are worn out it's time to buy an expensive new hub.

Regular maintenance of the bearings will help extend the life of the hub. Bearings need to be kept well adjusted, free of water and dirt, and well lubricated.

Gears

Gears are used to help us climb steep gradients, increase speed, or to maintain cadence (see p82). The concept is simple: large chainrings and small sprockets equal speed, while small chainrings and large sprockets make for easier climbing and faster acceleration.

Gear shifters

Shifters are used to change gear and on mountain bikes these are usually mounted on the handlebar, rather than on the down tube of the frame, as they are in most road bikes.

Index systems are almost universal on mountain bikes. They are characterised by their click-shift movement and there are three main types.

Thumbshifter: the original thumbshifter ('thumby') is mounted on top of the handlebar, alongside the brake lever, and activated by the thumb.

Rapidfire system: thumbies still have a large following, even though they have been superseded by the rapidfire system. In this system, the shifter is much closer to hand because the brake lever and shifter are combined into one unit.

Gripshifts: while arguments about the merits of the thumbshifter versus the rapidfire system were still raging, gripshift appeared on the scene, offering a throttle-like system for changing gear, built into the handle grip. Sceptics waited on the sidelines for problems

to appear but gripshifts have so far proved to be perfectly reliable and are increasingly popular and likely to be fitted as standard on the more deluxe mountain bikes.

Derailleurs

Gears are changed by derailing the chain from one gear cog so that it slips onto another. The sideways movement to do this is controlled by the derailleur, a simple-looking mechanism that requires very precise adjustment. If it gets clogged up with the mud and undergrowth that is easily picked up along the trail, it will soon stop working properly. Grit and mud picked up on the trail can also turn into a grinding paste that causes wear between the chain and gear, so it makes sense to keep the whole drive train clean and well lubricated.

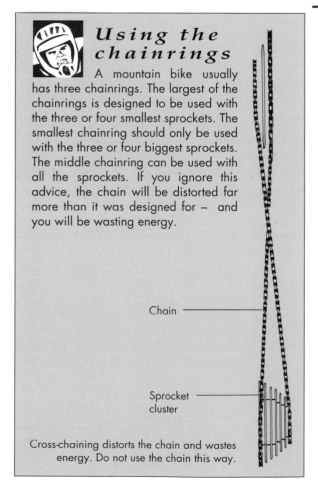

Using the chainrings

A mountain bike usually has three chainrings. The largest of the chainrings is designed to be used with the three or four smallest sprockets. The smallest chainring should only be used with the three or four biggest sprockets. The middle chainring can be used with all the sprockets. If you ignore this advice, the chain will be distorted far more than it was designed for – and you will be wasting energy.

Chain

Sprocket cluster

Cross-chaining distorts the chain and wastes energy. Do not use the chain this way.

DISHED WHEEL

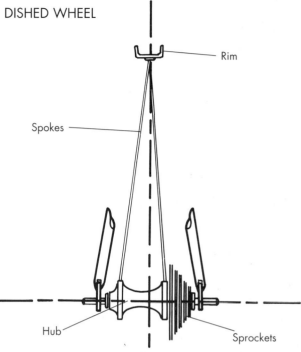

Rim

Spokes

Hub

Sprockets

Wheel dishing: as more gears are incorporated, the greater the dishing. For this reason, there is a limit to the number of gears a bike can have.

Gear ratios

The number of gears a bike has is no indication of how good it is. Mountain bikes commonly have 21 gears, and many now have 24. The only difference between the two is the narrowing of the gear ratios – the top and bottom gears remain the same. Narrowing the ratios (ie, closing the gap between the gears) makes the jump in pedal cadence smaller.

Another innovation is the micro drive, with its smaller chainrings, designed to save weight. Unfortunately they wear out faster.

Chainrings

Chainrings are usually made from steel, with aluminium alloy and titanium making lighter but more expensive options.

The smallest chainring is often of steel, even if the other two are not. This is because the teeth come round more often than on a larger ring so they are more liable to wear out – they also tend to be used in conditions of high wear.

The less expensive steel chainsets are made in one piece, with all three chainrings fixed to the spider and crankarm. If one chainring needs replacing you have to replace the lot, so this ends up not such a cheap alternative after all. With the better quality chainsets, each ring can be replaced individually.

Sprockets and rear derailleur

Most mountain bikes have seven rear sprockets, but eight-speed versions are now common. These may well represent the limit, given the current specification for wheel design and dropout width.

Sprockets are normally made of steel (often chrome treated). Hard-wearing titanium sprockets are also available, but they are hugely expensive. Aluminium alloy is rarely used on sprockets because it is not thought to be hard wearing enough. Even so, a few manufacturers have tried it, with good results.

Jockey wheels

Jockey wheels are the two plastic wheels that guide the chain round the rear derailleur mechanism. The jockey wheel bearings can wear unevenly if they get gunged up. They are easy to remove and keep clean. Do not be tempted to pack them with grease; this will only trap dirt and water.

If you are replacing Shimano jockey wheels, make sure the top wheel has a built-in play of $\frac{1}{32}$in (0.7mm) to allow for poor alignment; genuine Shimano parts have this important feature, but other manufacturers' parts may not.

Chain

A clean, well-lubricated chain is essential for long life and efficiency. A dirty chain will destroy itself, the chainrings and the sprockets. A dirty chain also means rougher gear changes.

Despite the varying claims of chain manufacturers, you should expect to replace a chain after every 2,000 miles (3,200 km) of road use. Off-road use will shorten a chain's life even further and in the most severe conditions a chain may only last 500 miles (800 km).

Chainring set up

● The teeth on each of the chainrings are of varying height, and there are small lugs on each of the rings. This is part of the design for better shifting. The side plates of the derailleur cage are also contoured to help with gear shifting. They need to be damage free and correctly located to work properly.

● With the large chainring selected, the derailleur outer cage plate should be $\frac{1}{32}$–$\frac{1}{8}$in (1–3 mm) above it. To adjust this, slacken the derailleur fixing on the seatpost. Ensure the chain cage is parallel with the chainrings. When in the correct position do not over-tighten the derailleur fixing, or you could crush the tubing. The only force on the derailleur should be the spring tension on the cable.

● When replacing the cable, shift the chain onto the smallest chainring. Turn the barrel adjuster clockwise all the way in, then back out two complete turns. With the cable in place pull it tight and tighten the cable clamp bolt (see section on replacing cables, page 42).

● On indexed gear-shift mechanisms, shift onto the middle chainring to adjust the derailleur. Use the barrel adjuster on the shifter to position the cage so that it doesn't brush against the chain in any of the gears.

● To prevent the chain from being derailed too far in either direction adjust the limit screws. The outer screw adjusts the outer chainring; the inner screw the inner chainring. If you can't get onto the small chainring, even when the adjuster is fully out, the cable is probably too tight. Slacken off the cable using the barrel adjuster on the shifter.

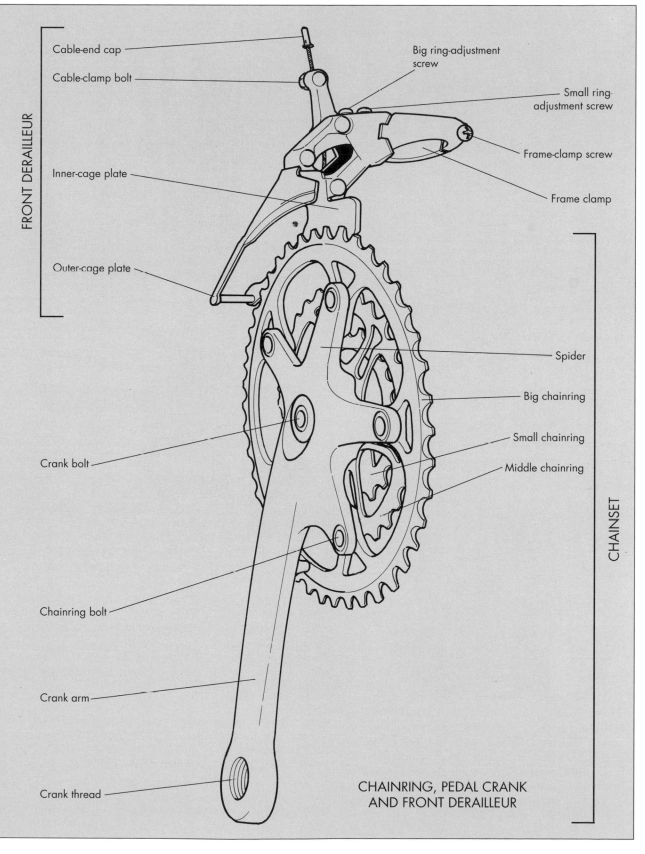

Cable-end cap

Cable-clamp bolt

Inner-cage plate

Outer-cage plate

Big ring-adjustment screw

Small ring-adjustment screw

Frame-clamp screw

Frame clamp

Spider

Big chainring

Small chainring

Middle chainring

Crank bolt

Chainring bolt

Crank arm

Crank thread

CHAINSET

CHAINRING, PEDAL CRANK
AND FRONT DERAILLEUR

Rear derailleur set up

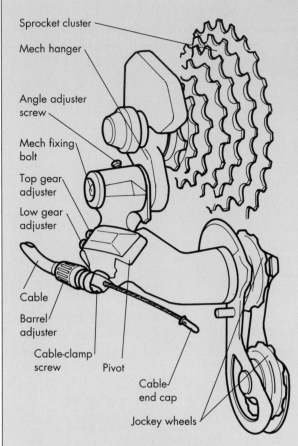

Sprocket cluster

Mech hanger

Angle adjuster screw

Mech fixing bolt

Top gear adjuster

Low gear adjuster

Cable

Barrel adjuster

Cable-clamp screw

Pivot

Cable end cap

Jockey wheels

Sprockets and jockey wheels on the rear derailleur

1. To make sure the chain doesn't fall off the top or bottom sprocket, you need to adjust the derailleur stops. Shift onto the largest sprocket and screw the lower of the two screws on the back of the derailler mechanism inwards (clockwise) until it starts to push the chain off the sprocket. Now unscrew it until the top jockey wheel is directly under the sprocket.

2. Now shift the chain onto the smallest sprocket and screw the top stop in until the chain touches the second sprocket. Unscrew the stop until it clears the second sprocket.

3. Indexed gear shifters need to be set up carefully to work properly. With both Suntour and Shimano gear systems, adjustments are simply made using the barrel at the end of the gear cable, where it joins the derailleur mechanism.

On a Shimano system, shift the chain onto the second-smallest sprocket. If there is too much slack in the cable, turn the barrel adjuster anticlockwise to move the mechanism across. On the second sprocket, screw the adjuster out (anticlockwise) until the chain touches the third sprocket and starts to 'chatter' as you rotate the pedals.

Now screw the adjuster back in (clockwise) a quarter of a turn. Next try shifting between the sprockets a few times. If the chain is reluctant to shift to a larger sprocket, turn the barrel adjuster half a turn anticlockwise. If the chain is reluctant to shift to a smaller sprocket, turn the barrel adjuster half a turn clockwise.

Follow the same routine on Suntour systems but start with the chain on the smallest sprocket.

4. To position the top jockey wheel in relation to the sprockets, use the tension screw at the top of the derailleur where it butts up to the rear of the hanger. Shift the chain onto the largest sprocket and the smallest chainring. Adjust the screw so that the top jockey wheel is as close to the sprocket as possible without actually touching.

Now shift the chain onto the smallest sprocket and the largest chainring. If the top jockey wheel is touching the sprocket, adjust the screw until it is clear. If you find changing to a larger sprocket is difficult, then the jockey wheel is too close. If, when you change to a smaller sprocket, it jumps two, then the jockey wheel is too far away.

Tools: screwdriver.
Parts: if replacing the gear cable, new cable, lubricant and cable-end caps.

Replacing the gear cable: If you are replacing the gear cable, shift the chain onto the smallest sprocket. Screw the barrel adjusters in a clockwise direction on both the gear shifter and the derailleur. Now unscrew the shifter barrel two full turns and the derailleur barrel one full turn. Pull the cable tight and tighten the cable clamp bolt (see section on replacing cables, page 42).

(see section on replacing cables, page 42).

Shimano compatibility

Shimano is the name of a Japanese company that manufactures nearly all of the bicycle components sold in Europe and North America. It is a name that you will come across frequently in this book, because their components are fitted to virtually all mountain bikes, unless you specify something different.

Many manufacturers produce cassettes, sprockets, shifters and derailleurs that are Shimano compatible. Suntour parts should be checked for compatibility with Shimano systems before fitting. As a general rule Shimano and Suntour derailleurs and shifters should not be mixed.

Chains get longer as they wear, and it is easy to gauge how much wear a chain has sustained. Since each link is 1 inch (2.54 cm) long, 12 links should measure 12 inches (30.5 cm). If they measure 12$\frac{1}{16}$ inch (34.5 cm) the chain is getting worn.

As a general rule, you should change the sprockets every time you change the chain. You might get away with this once if you are

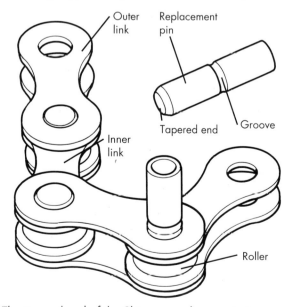

The tapered end of the Shimano replacement pin serves as a guide to allow the pin to be lined up before being pressed home. The groove ensures that the pin breaks in the right place.

Changing a chain

Tools: chainbreaker (Shimano Hyperglide chains need a special chain breaker). Pliers for breaking off Hyperglide connecting pin.

Parts: new chain. Hyperglide chain needs special connecting pin.

1. Check the chain for wear. It should be replaced when it has stretched by as much as ¹⁄₁₆ inch (2 mm) over 12 inches (30.5 cm), which is 12 links. You can use a steel ruler to check for wear, but a special chain-checker tool, such as the one shown above, will make the task a lot easier.

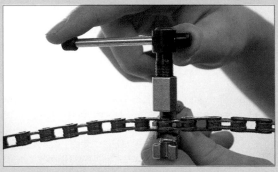

3. To rejoin the chain place it back in the chain tool and drive the pin back through. If it sticks, twist the links a bit to line up the pin and holes. When the pin is just proud of the plate, put the chain in the spreader slot. Drive the pin a quarter to a third of a turn, until it is level with the other pins. This will spread the link and prevent stiffness. If it is still stiff, try flexing the chain from side to side to free it off.

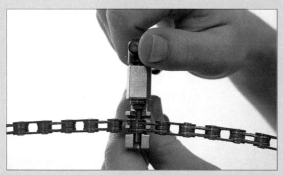

2. Rest the chain in the chain tool. Make sure it is held firmly in place by screwing the handle in. With the chain correctly positioned, turn the handle 5½ full turns. On normal chains this will be enough to split the chain. You do not want the chain pin to be pushed all the way out. If the chain does not split, give it another half turn or so until it comes apart. Ideally the pin should remain slightly proud of the inside of the outer plate. This will make it easier to rejoin the plate.

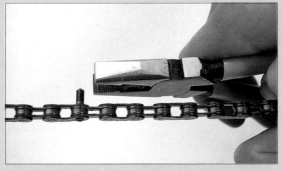

4. Shimano chains are different as they require their own special chain tool. Drive the pin all the way out. To rejoin the link, use the special black Shimano replacement pin (see page 35), which is pointed at one end and oversized to accommodate the hole enlargement. Push the narrow end through the two links to be joined. Use the chain tool to drive the pin all the way through until the groove in the pin emerges. You will hear a click and the pressure eases. Don't drive it through any more or you'll start to enlarge the side-plate hole. Break off the projecting part of the pin with pliers. Do not break the chain at this point again, because one oversized pin cannot be replaced with another.

Chain fitting

The best place to work on the chain is under the chain stay rather than above – this way, the chain is less likely to undo itself if you have to let go. The jockey-wheel arm has a tendency to pull the chain out of the chain tool. You can avoid this by removing the chain from the chainring. If you still need more slack, try tying the jockey-wheel cage to the chain stay. When putting the chain back, make sure it is threaded properly through the jockey wheels, front derailleur cage and the chain stay.

very careful and change the chain before it wears any more. If you let the chain stretch to 12⅛ inch (35 cm) it is very likely that you will have to change the sprockets too. The chain will stretch from 1/16 inch to 1/8 inch in a fraction of the time it took to stretch the first 1/16.

If the sprockets aren't changed at the same time as a badly worn chain the new chain is likely to slip around the sprockets. When replacing a chain or a sprocket set, you may want to upgrade to lightweight components, but do check that the new chain or sprocket set is compatible with your existing components – not all are interchangeable. Chrome chains are claimed to last longer and give better gear shifting.

Bottom bracket

The bottom bracket is the part of the frame that houses the spindle and bearings for the pedal cranks, enabling power to be transmitted via the pedals and chainring to the chain. The pedal cranks are fitted to the ends of a spindle that is supported on bearings housed within the bike frame.

The chainring crank pedal acts directly on the chainring, while the other crank uses the spindle to transfer power to the chainring. The spindle connecting the two cranks can be made of steel or titanium; titanium is lighter, but claims that it is stronger are not totally proven.

The spindle suffers stress from the twisting motion of energy being transferred along its length and the bending that results from

weight being applied to it from the pedal. The effect of this is to waste energy and increase stress on the spindle.

These effects can be reduced by shortening the spindle length and shortening the distance from the crank arm to the bearings. Although you may be able to improve the placement of bearings in a replacement part it is not really practicable to reduce the spindle length.

Bottom brackets come in two forms: the traditional cup-and-cones type, and the more recent sealed cartridge. The cup-and-cones bracket is easy to maintain but needs more attention than a sealed cartridge unit and will eventually need to be replaced. When that time comes, the axle will need replacing too.

Most people choose this moment to replace their cup-and-cone bracket with a new sealed cartridge, and most bike manufacturers now fit cartridge bottom brackets as standard.

Servicing cup-and-cone brackets

On a cup-and-cone bottom bracket, unscrew the lockring on the non-drive side and then, using a peg spanner, remove the cup. Now unscrew the fixed cup on the drive side.

Inspect the cups and axle. Replace the entire assembly if any parts show wear. As a matter of course it is best to replace the old bearings, even if you are not replacing the cups and cones. Clean the cups and axle, pack the cups with grease, and seat the new bearings inside the cup. Screw the fixed cone tightly into the bottom bracket shell on the drive side.

With the axle in position, screw the adjustable cup into the non-drive side of the shell until the bearings start to bind. Screw on the lockring and tighten it against the bracket shell, holding the cup in place. This tightening against the bracket shell pulls the cup out very slightly, releasing the binding of the bearings. You may need to do a bit of fine tuning until there is no play or binding left in the bearing.

When removing the bottom bracket, brute strength is often required, after you have first soaked the threads with penetrating oil. When putting everything back together, take care not to get the component threads crossed; every-

Bottom bracket cartridge replacement

Tools: Allen key or spanner for crank bolt removal. Crank puller and adjustable spanner to remove cranks from axle. Peg spanner or special tool, depending on design, for removing cartridge bottom brackets.

Parts: New bearings. New cups to replace pitted cups. If axle is pitted and needs replacement then consider upgrading to a sealed unit. If the sealed unit is worn, replace with new sealed unit.

A special tool is needed to remove cartridge bottom brackets: check that you have one before you start.

1. Remove the pedal cranks. After taking out the retaining bolt, a crank extractor will be needed to get the crank arms off the tapered axle.

3. Before reassembly, clean out the bottom bracket shell. You will probably be surprised by the muck, rust and water that is visible here once the bearing is removed. Most of this dirt will have entered the frame down the seat tube. Clean the shell and grease the shell threads.

2. Use the special bottom-bracket tool to unscrew the non-drive side first (anticlockwise) and then the drive side (clockwise). When you unscrew the drive side, the whole cartridge comes out.

4. To fit a new cartridge, simply screw the large cartridge piece into the drive-side, until it is tight and the lip is against the frame. Now screw the smaller cup into the non-drive side, using the bottom-bracket tool to make sure that it is tight.

thing should screw back together gently, without too much effort. If not, then check that all the threads are clean and well greased. If the bottom bracket shell threads are badly rusted or damaged consider getting your local bike shop to tap out the threads.

Some bottom bracket manufacturers recommend that the bottom-bracket shell should be faced (smoothed and levelled) before fitting a new bottom bracket. Facing ensures that the bearings are in proper alignment to prevent undue wear.

Before refitting the cranks, check the chainrings for wear; this is a good opportunity for replacement.

Brakes

Mountain bike brakes use a simple cantilever design, unlike other bikes, which usually have side-pull brakes. Cantilever brakes continue to operate effectively in muddy conditions, and are less prone to clogging. Good brakes allow you to make faster descents and give better control in poor conditions. It is possible to wear a set of brake blocks out very quickly so it is important that you know how to set up and adjust your brakes properly.

Brake blocks

Keep brake blocks clean of grit and mud, as these increase the wear on both the brake blocks and the wheel rims. Shimano cartridge replacement blocks are a recent development that separates the block from the stud. Replacement blocks are slid into a holder and secured by a bolt.

Brake pads come in various lengths; as a rule, the longer they are, the better. Brake blocks made from soft compounds give better braking but don't last long.

Change your brake blocks before they wear to the bottom of the grooves. Below that lurks a metal rivet that will gouge out your rim.

If brake blocks get overheated the surface becomes glazed and doesn't work properly. Sanding the surface down will cure this, but don't overdo it.

CANTILEVER BRAKES

A well-adjusted cantilever brake has an angle of 90 degrees between the arms and the cable.

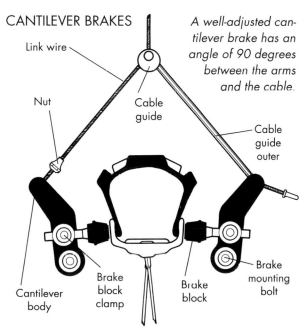

Link wire

Nut

Cable guide

Cable guide outer

Cantilever body

Brake block clamp

Brake block

Brake mounting bolt

BRAKE TOE-IN

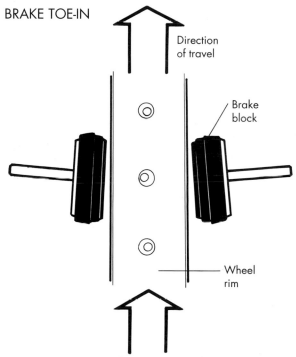

Direction of travel

Brake block

Wheel rim

As the brake pads grip the rim, they are pulled in the direction of travel. 'Toe-in' compensates for this and ensures the whole block sits flush against the rim when the brakes are applied.

Servicing cantilever brakes

1. Cantilever brakes are easy enough to dismantle and clean. Worn brake blocks should be replaced and the cantilever boss and spring should be lubricated. Before replacing the brakes, clean the wheel rim and check for damage and buckling (see page 23 on truing a wheel).

When you refit the cantilever arm to the pivot on the bike frame, take care not to overtighten the pivot bolts as this will cause the boss to splay and the pivot to bind. Make sure the spring is seated correctly in the cantilever arm. The spring normally sits in the middle of the three holes on the boss.

2. Fit new brake blocks, making sure they point in the correct direction. Refit the straddle cable. Position the blocks so they rest squarely on the rim. The block studs should be horizontal or with the wheel end slightly higher as cantilever brakes have a tendency to ride down the rim towards the spokes when the brakes are applied.

Cable upgrade

Gore-tex RideOn cable systems are the best available and they require little maintenance. These have a coated inner wire, which passes through a low-friction liner which itself goes inside the housing cable. Cables, liners and housings are not interchangeable with other systems, however.

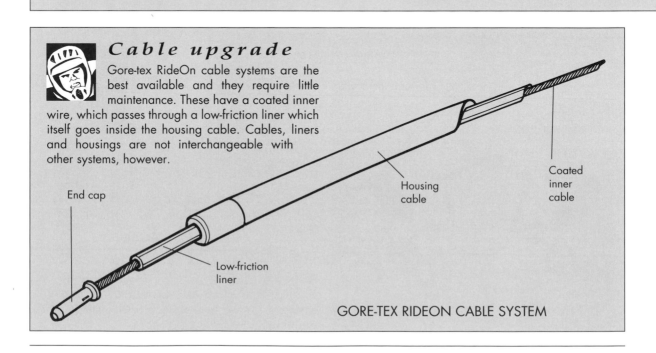

End cap

Low-friction liner

Housing cable

Coated inner cable

GORE-TEX RIDEON CABLE SYSTEM

3. Adjust the brake blocks so that the front edge of the block almost touches the wheel, while the rear edge has a ³⁄₃₂ in (2 mm) gap. A piece of card trapped between the rim and the block will help you get this right (this adjustment is known as toeing in, and it stops the blocks squealing when the brakes are applied – see diagram on page 39).

4. Use the barrel adjuster to ensure the brake blocks clear the rim by ³⁄₃₂in (2 mm). Adjust the spring balance to ensure that the brake pads are an equal distance from the wheel rim and therefore strike the rim together.

Tighten all fixings. Test the brakes by applying hard pressure and rocking the bike back and forth a few times.

Tools: spanners and/or Allen key.

Parts: new blocks. Make sure the block compound suits your riding style and the expected nature of the terrain.

To ensure that the brakes work effectively, the angle between the two cables running from the bridge to the cantilever arm should be about 90 degrees. Often it is around 100 degrees. At 90 degrees more force is transmitted along the cable. Altering these angles will change the ratio of brake lever travel to the force applied to the rim. A more positive feel can also be obtained, with less brake-lever movement, by decreasing the bridge wire angle and increasing the angle between the cantilever arm and the cable.

Straddle-cable and link-wire brakes

Cantilever brakes come in two forms. The straddle-cable type has a cable that stretches between the cantilever arms of the two brakes. This cable loops over a yoke attached to the brake cable and, as the yoke rises, the straddle cable is pulled up, applying the brakes.

The Shimano link-wire system is a slightly more sophisticated version of the same thing. Here, the main brake cable passes through a cable guide to one of its cantilevers, while the other cantilever is operated by a link wire passing from the cable guide to the other brake.

Other types of brakes

As well as the two cantilever brake systems, there are several types of brake that can be fitted to mountain bikes, though it is unlikely that these will find their way onto mass-produced bikes until the costs are brought down.
Disc brakes: the disc is located in the centre of the wheel, making the spokes take all the stress. These are expensive to buy and maintain, and rather heavy, but they give very good stopping in all conditions and don't get clogged in mud.

Cable replacement

Tools: spanner or Allen key, depending on fixings. Wire cutters. Pliers. Third-hand tools to hold cable in position (you can manage without it).

Parts: new inner cables (and outers if these are being replaced too). Cable inner and outer end caps.

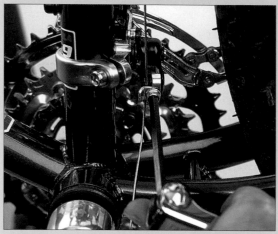

1. Before removing inner gear cables, shift the gears onto the smallest cogs to relieve the tension. Remove the cable-end cap and undo the retaining bolt.

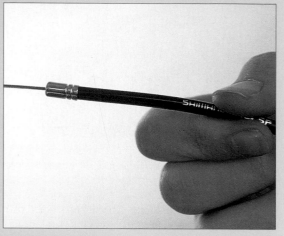

3. Thread the new cable through the brake lever or shifter, and then through the outer cable. Slot the outer cables back into their slots.

2. Remove any cable-end covers on the gear shifters. Push the inner cable through until it emerges from the brake lever or the gear shifter. Draw the inner cable all the way out.

4. Thread the cable through the clamp bolt on the brake lever or derailleur mechanism. Pull it until all the slack has been removed and tighten the clamp bolt. Finally cut off the excess cable, leaving 1 in (2.5 cm) of cable, and fit a cable-end cap. Some cantilever brake arms have a hook to wrap the cable end behind.

Drum brakes: these have similar disadvantages to disc brakes and are difficult to set up.
Hydraulic rim brakes: these are expensive and unkind to rims. They are also very powerful and require little maintenance.

> ### Cable length and travel
> Use your old cables as a yardstick for judging how long the replacements should be. Make sure you have allowed for the full travel of the handlebars to left and right. Make sure that none of the cable curves is too tight, as the cables will bind. Always fit cable-end caps.

Cables

Cables are used to control the brakes and the gears. Damage to the cables can seriously affect the bike's performance, so you need to keep them clean and lubricated. If they are allowed to get dirty or rusty they will bind inside the outer cable, and if the cable doesn't slide smoothly, the gear change suffers.

When cleaning or adjusting gear cables, shift the gears onto the smallest ring. This will take the tension off the cable. It is possible to lubricate and clean the cables without disconnecting them. Clean off all visible dirt from the exposed inner cables and the outer sheath. Pull the outer cables from their stops. You can now pull the inner cables from the outer cover to clean and lubricate the previously hidden cable. Be careful not to let muck get drawn into the inner cable in the process.

A better job can be made if the cables are undone and the outers completely removed. Use spray lubricant to clean the insides of the outer cables. It is often recommended that grease be applied to the cables. It should be used sparingly because water can easily become trapped inside, and muck will stick to the grease and work its way inside the outer cable. A dry teflon-based lubricant is best for this purpose. If you are replacing cables, use the low-friction teflon-coated variety. When replacing outer cables, choose the lateral wire construction type, such as the Shimano SIS. Helical cables are not such a good alternative because they compress slightly every time you tension the cable; this will lead to loss of precision when changing gear.

Handlebars

The handlebar assembly undergoes a great deal more stress and strain than is generally realized, and some of the newer lightweight versions can snap without warning. Carbon-fibre handlebars are most liable to fail, whilst the strongest bars are titanium, by a large margin. Titanium bars are also the most expensive, so most people go for a compromise between cost and strength, choosing chromoly steel or aluminium alloy.

The main stress point on the handlebar assembly is the clamp, the circular tube into which the handlebar is fitted and which runs from the handlebar to the stem. Most handlebars are bulged at this point for added strength. Bear in mind that, if you choose narrow handlebars, the bulge will take up quite a bit of the length, leaving little space for mounting extra components, such as gear levers, computers, carriers and the like.

HANDLE BAR CLAMP

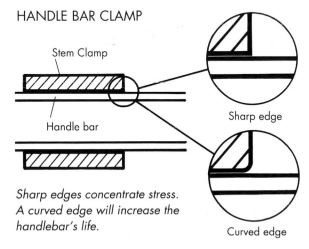

Sharp edges concentrate stress. A curved edge will increase the handlebar's life.

Handlebar grips

Handlebar grips should give a firm feel and absorb shock without being too soft. Some riders suffer from numb or sleepy hands while

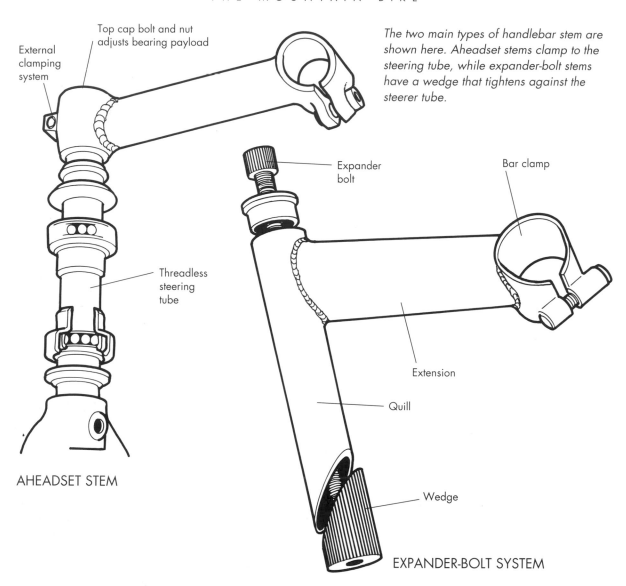

External clamping system

Top cap bolt and nut adjusts bearing payload

The two main types of handlebar stem are shown here. Aheadset stems clamp to the steering tube, while expander-bolt stems have a wedge that tightens against the steerer tube.

Threadless steering tube

Expander bolt

Bar clamp

Extension

Quill

Wedge

AHEADSET STEM

EXPANDER-BOLT SYSTEM

Sizing the handlebars

The handlebars should be level with the seat or up to 3 in (7.5 cm) lower.

The width of the handlebars should never be narrower than the rider's shoulders. Most people find that their shoulder width added to the width of both hands is the widest they need. Narrow bars are lighter but more difficult to hold when an obstacle is struck. Wider bars get caught up in undergrowth.

If you want to shorten the bar use a tube cutter, not a hacksaw. Sawing can start off tiny cracks in aluminium and titanium that can lead to early bar failure.

Never use a bent handlebar or try straightening it.

End plugs should always be fitted to handlebars and bare tube ends. Bare tube ends make a neat hole in human flesh, which is likely to happen if you crash.

When buying handlebars make sure that there are no burrs or sharp edges around the clamp. Scratches from burrs can set up stress lines and lead to early failure, as can sharp edges.

riding, a condition known as Carpal Tunnel Syndrome. This is caused by pressure on the nerves in the palm of the hand. Using softer grips can aggravate the condition because riders tend to grip harder, thus putting more pressure on the palm of the hand.

Getting grips off

To remove grips that have stuck, lift the edge and spray lubricant underneath. Twisting the grip backwards and forwards will work in the lube and release the grip.

Handlebar stems

Stems are often overlooked, but they control the rider's reach and are therefore very important when you are trying to get the most comfortable riding position. When buying a handlebar assembly, therefore, you need to check that the handlebar length and angle is right for your body size.

The materials most commonly used for stems are aluminium and chromoly steel. The bar clamp can be secured either by a single bolt or by lighter double bolts. Some assemblies also have a cable hanger attached which is used for supporting the front brake cable.

Headsets

The biggest difference you will find between stems is in the headset fitting. This is the fitting that connects the handlebar stem to the front fork assembly via the steerer tube. There are two types: the Aheadset stem and the expander-bolt stem.

The expander-bolt type has a bolt running through the stem to a wedge (known as the quill) at the base of the stem. Tightening the bolt draws the wedge tight up against the inside of the steerer tube. Some lightweight versions have a shortened expander bolt which is recessed deep inside the stem.

Keep the expander bolt and wedge well greased. If the stem doesn't come free when the expander bolt is loosened gently tap the bolt. (see page 46 for headset).

Aheadset stems clamp onto longer steerer tubes. The benefit is that weight is saved by doing away with the wedge, quill and expander bolt. Aheadset stems are attached to the steerer tube by means of two bolts. Some systems have bolts flush with the stem to avoid injuries from protruding bolts.

Saddle

Comfort should be the over-riding factor when choosing a saddle – and comfort is far more important than weight saving. It is no good getting a light saddle if it is uncomfortable. The latest in this area is the gel saddle which, though heavier, is supposed to mould to the rider for increased comfort. There are also saddles especially designed for women, whose pelvic bones are wider than those of a man, and therefore need proper support.

Seat posts

The traditional seat post has a clamp to hold the saddle. The bottom part of the clamp is curved and serrated and it sits in a matching curved serrated cradle. A single bolt holds them altogether. A groove in the cradle allows the two serrated faces to be adjusted to alter the seat angle.

The other type of seat post in common use is known as the micro-adjusting post. This holds the seat in a non-serrated cradle and allows for finer adjustments than are possible with the serrated version.

The angle of the saddle is a matter of personal preference. Tilting it forward from the level will put more weight on your arms, shoulders and back. Tilting it back can lead to discomfort because your arms and shoulders will be stretched.

Aluminium alloy is the most favoured material in seatposts. Chromoly, carbonfibre and titanium can also be used. When aluminium alloy seatposts are used with a steel seat tube, galvanic corrosion can fuse the two together. Always replace a bent seatpost.

Keep the seat post well greased; this will stop water getting into the seat tube and prevent corrosion.

Headset care

Tools: locknut spanners, screwdriver, Allen key, degreaser.

Parts: new bearings, plastic cap (aheadsets only), neoprene seals or scraps of inner tube.

Headsets have two sets of bearings, located at each end of the head tube. These bearings take a lot of abuse. Faults in the headset are tight spots, grinding, and clunking when the brakes are applied.

1. After removing the stem from the head tube, slacken the headset locknuts. Hold the bottom cup nut with a spanner while undoing the top locknut. A lot of force is required to get the first bit of movement. Remove the locknut and any washers, spacers or seals, laying them down on a clean surface in their correct order, and then remove the bearing cup. Support the bike so that the forks do not fall out of the tube; if this happens, the bearings tend to go everywhere and get lost. Instead, lower the forks gently from the headtub, and take out the bearings carefully.

2. Degrease and thoroughly clean all the components. Check all parts for wear. It is usual to replace bearings as a matter of course, but you will definitely have to if any are pittedor worn. If the cups and cones are pitted or dented, then replace ther entire headset. If you do this, make sure that the new headset is aligned properly. This may require the attentions of a skilled bike mechanic.

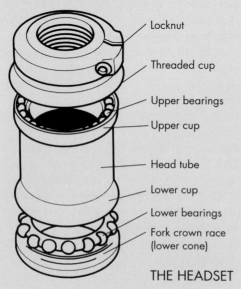

Locknut

Threaded cup

Upper bearings

Upper cup

Head tube

Lower cup

Lower bearings

Fork crown race
(lower cone)

THE HEADSET

3. Headset bearings are usually purchased as a set, in a cage. If you want, you can dispense with the cage and fit extra bearings into the greased bearing cup, so as to spread the load on the bearings. Roller bearings are used in more expensive headsets and give a larger bearing surface area than ball bearings. They come in a cage to keep them in the correct position and won't work without it.

4. Aheadsets have a different set-up on the top bearing. Remove the adjuster bolt and cap. Loosen the stem clamps. Remove the stem and any spacers. On some forks there is a circlip above the top bearing that also needs to be removed. This keeps everything together when the stem is removed.

6. On the aheadset only, lightly oil the contact surfaces between the top bearing and the circular wedge above it. Make sure the stem moves freely on the steerer tube before adjusting the bearings. With the bike off the ground, tighten the adjuster bolt until the bearings just bind, then slacken it off slightly. There should be no play or binding. Now tighten the stem clamp.

5. Before reassembly, lightly grease the stem and all the threads. Make sure that there is plenty of grease in the bearings. When reassembling the headset, tighten the cone nut until the bearings just start to bind, then screw the locknut down on top of the cone nut until the locknut is just tight. Holding the locknut in place turn the cone nut back tight onto the locknut. If you have got the last bit right, the bearings should turn smoothly without binding or any play. If not, try again. It may take one or two attempts to get this spot-on. Some headsets have a locking mechanism to keep the locknut tight using an Allen bolt. It is possible to buy these locknuts as separate items.

Notes :
- Remember the position of any washers or seals.
- Don't mix the bearings from the top and bottom.
- The plastic cap on the top of an aheadset is specially designed to break if too much force is exerted, so don't replace it with one other than from the original manufacturer.
- Neoprene seals are available to go over the bottom bearing to keep water out. Some people use a piece of inner tube as a cheap substitute.

Seatposts come in various diameters, so make sure that any replacements are of the correct size. The post should slide easily in and out of the seat tube and clamp without distorting the clamp or bolt.

Never extend the post beyond the seat marker. If your frame has an extended seat tube, make sure there is at least 2 in (50 mm) of seat post below the seat cluster (ie below the junction of the seat post and the top tube).

Avoid scratches to the seat tube by removing any sharp edges on the frame with a file.

An inner tube can be rolled over the seat tube to cover the clamp and keep out water and dirt. Seat clamps either come as part of

Adjusting the stem

Limit marks on the stem tube show how far it is safe to heighten the handlebars. Never adjust the stem so that the limit marks show, or the handlebar assembly could snap, causing a nasty accident.

Prise open clamps with a large screwdriver. Never use a twisting action to push the handlebars through. This causes scratches that weaken the tube structure. Tighten the clamps just enough to stop the handlebar from moving. If you overdo the pressure you will crush the tube.

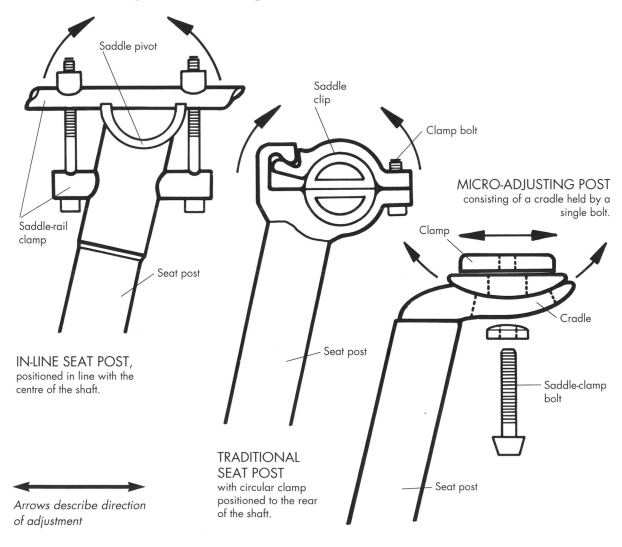

Saddle pivot

Saddle-rail clamp

Seat post

IN-LINE SEAT POST,
positioned in line with the centre of the shaft.

Arrows describe direction of adjustment

Saddle clip

Clamp bolt

Seat post

TRADITIONAL SEAT POST
with circular clamp positioned to the rear of the shaft.

MICRO-ADJUSTING POST
consisting of a cradle held by a single bolt.

Clamp

Cradle

Saddle-clamp bolt

Seat post

the frame or as separate items positioned at either the front or the back of the tube. A clamp at the front of the tube will not let as much muck and water into the seat tube as one at the rear.

Quick-release or Allen bolts can be used to secure the seat post. Quick-release bolts are good for making running adjustments, especially on downhill runs, but they also make life easier for thieves.

Pedals

Pedals tend to be forgotten, perhaps because of the fiddly nature of the servicing that is required. Difficult as this is, pedals should not be neglected, because they are the first link in the chain that transfers energy from your legs to the rear wheels of your bike.

Pedals come in two forms: ordinary pedals (which should be fitted with toe clips or half clips) and heavier clip-in pedals (known as clipless pedals or SPDs).

To use clip-in pedals, the rider needs to wear a special shoe with a cleat in the sole that fits into a clip in the pedal. Clip-in systems (plus shoes) therefore cost more, but they provide a stiffer platform for the foot, and so waste less energy. They have a tendency to clog with mud, but this is not as bad a problem as is often suggested. In fact, it is only a problem if you are using the bike in conditions where mud, grit or other debris stops the mechanism working properly.

Ordinary pedals are better if you are riding in conditions that require a lot of getting off and carrying, especially if you want to wear walking boots on your feet, for extra support

Straps

Adjust the toe strap so that the buckle is positioned near the cage (rather than near the toe strap) on the outside of the pedal. Use a zip tie to fasten the strap securely to the cage. This will prevent the strap from moving, and will allow dirt to fall through.

and grip. Either way, it is easy to change the pedals back and forth, choosing the best type for the conditions you expect to encounter.

Float

Float is the built-in movement on clip-in pedals that allows your feet to move in the pedal without coming out of the clip.

Conventional pedals

Conventional pedals must be easy to lubricate, so make sure that the cage on which your foot sits can be removed easily. Alternatively, if the cage is not removable, check to see if the pedal has grease ports that allow for the insertion of grease without dismantling the pedal.

Aluminium alloy, steel, carbonfibre and titanium are all used in pedals. The weight versus price choice is yours, but remember that the heavier the pedal, the more energy is required to move it.

Servicing conventional pedals

Remove the pedals from the crank arm (remember that the left-hand pedal unscrews clockwise, and the right-hand pedal unscrews anticlockwise). You may have to remove the cage and the toe clips in order to get at the bearing dust cap. It is difficult to avoid damaging the dust cap when removing it. Hold the pedal axle in a soft-jawed vice or even an adjustable spanner. A special socket is needed to remove the locknut. Next, remove the tabbed washer (this can be fiddly). Place a flat-bladed screwdriver between the cone and the pedal body. Turn the axle to undo the cone.

Clean and degrease all the parts. Check the bearing surfaces for wear in the form of pitting and dents. If they are badly worn, the pedal should be replaced. It is a good idea to replace the bearings every time you service the pedals.

Place the new bearings in a shallow bed of grease on the bearing surface. Without dislodging the bearings apply more grease on to the top surface of the bearings. Put the axle back in the pedal body, making sure it seats

properly. Refit the cone nut, tab washer and locknut. Tighten the locknut using the screwdriver until there is minimal play. Now tighten the locknut fully. The axle should turn freely without any play. If not, adjust the locknut and cone nut again.

Pack the dust cap and outer bearing with grease. Push the dust cap on. Refit the cages and toe straps. Before screwing the pedal back onto the crank, clean and grease the threads.

Clip-in pedals

The most common clip-in pedal system is called Shimano Pedalling Dynamics (otherwise known as SPDs). There are two main types of SPDs: both have double-sided pedals and use the same shoe cleats, and both require the cleat to be twisted to remove it from the pedal. The difference lies in the hinges on the pedals. The PD-M737 (XT) version has hinges at the front and the rear of the pedal, allowing the rider to stand on the pedal to engage it. The PD-M535 (DX) is a lighter and cheaper version that only has one hinge. The rider has to slide the cleat under a catch plate before pressing on the rear hinge to engage the cleat fully. This version has fewer moving parts and works better in the mud. Cleats and body plates need to be replaced, however, as they get worn.

Servicing clip-in pedals

To service SPDs, remove them from the crank (clockwise for the left-hand pedal, anticlockwise for the right-hand pedal). Remove the axle, using the special tool which is usually provided when you buy SPDs. Clean all the surfaces. The end of the axle has a cone and locknut which can be used to adjust the bearing. Slacken off the locknut and turn the cone nut until there is no play and the bearing turns freely. Half fill the pedal body with grease and refit the spindle. This forces the grease through the bearing. Although it is possible to change the bearings, most people prefer to replace the entire spindle, complete with bearings.

(LEFT) Loose clips and cages on the pedal can be irritating, so take tools to carry out running repairs.

Suspension

The most noticeable advance in bike design in recent years is the introduction of suspension. On tough terrain this can completely change the character of the ride. Not only does suspension take the bumps out of the ride, it also lets you ride rough terrain faster. In fact, it will not be long before your rides become just as tricky as they were without suspension – because you will be travelling so much faster that you may be tempted to ride to the limit of your ability.

Suspension systems work through a combination of springs and dampers. The springs absorb the force and can be made of coiled steel or elastomer rubber, though air can also be used to act as an impact cushion.

Damping is what stops the suspension springs bouncing you around too much. On an elastomer fork the damping is also performed by the elastomer. Air and steel-spring systems use oil damping which is achieved by forcing oil through tubes or holes.

Oil damping is affected by the viscosity of the oil and the diameter of the hole it is forced through. The best combination is a low viscosity oil with smaller diameter channels. To get the ride that suits you best you will need to experiment with the thickness and viscosity of the oil you use.

You should also keep an eye on fluid levels. If the oil level is too high, pressure can increase in the unit and stop it responding properly. If the oil level gets too low, friction will increase the wear and seals may dry out, causing leakage. Should this occur the problem might remedy itself when the oil level is restored, but don't rely on it – you may need to replace the seals, which is a specialist task.

Front fork suspension

Suspension forks have two different sized components that slide one inside the other. The upper tube fixed to the bike is called the stanchion while the other tube is known as the slider. Not all forks are fitted to the bike in the same way. Some have the sliders at the top while others have them at the bottom.

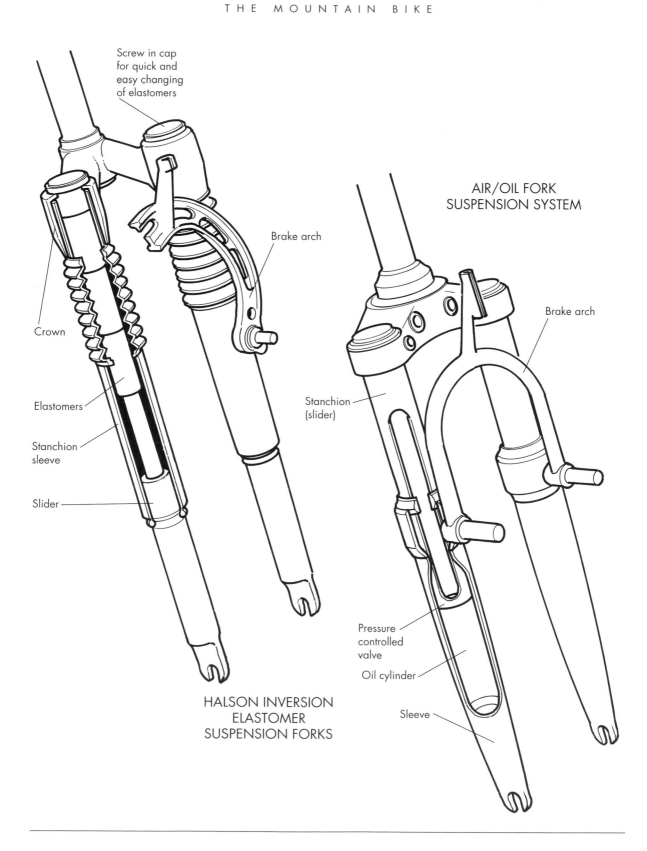

Screw in cap for quick and easy changing of elastomers

Brake arch

AIR/OIL FORK
SUSPENSION SYSTEM

Crown

Brake arch

Elastomers

Stanchion
(slider)

Stanchion
sleeve

Slider

Pressure
controlled
valve

Oil cylinder

HALSON INVERSION
ELASTOMER
SUSPENSION FORKS

Sleeve

Where the sliders are positioned at the top of the unit they tend to be a lot heavier. On lower-quality forks this extra weight can reduce efficiency. Although not as popular, sliders positioned at the bottom of the fork are a lot lighter. By placing the extra weight of the sleeves above the springs, you increase the suspension efficiency.

Flex

Forks do not just move up and down: they also twist around. This torsional flex is undesirable. To reduce this effect requires well-made fork braces and a firm front-axle assembly. This has led to the design of front-suspension hubs that have a larger face to prevent flex. Before buying a front-suspension hub, check that it will fit your forks. You also need a steel front-hub skewer that can be tightened well. Good hub setup is more important where the sleeve is part of the lower fork.

Other fork designs

A few manufacturers use a normal fork, but with a single suspension unit fitted above the fork crown. These systems have compatibility problems and cannot always be fitted to existing wheels and frames. They also require more maintenance than purpose-designed suspension forks.

Rear suspension

Rear suspension systems have not yet been perfected. The currently favoured system is based on a swing arm that pivots on the bike frame and holds the rear wheel. Sticking this arm onto the rear of the bike introduces some unwelcome side effects.

Apart from the extra flex that a swing arm introduces over the traditional rear triangle, there are two other concerns. One is that some of the peddling force is wasted on the suspension system. The other is pedal feedback caused by the fact that the pivot point is separate from the centre of the bottom bracket.

Multi-pivot designs have been developed that can control pedal feedback very well. The disadvantage is the side loading on the swing arm, which is a considerable source of wear on the pivots, wear that is increased by any muck picked up on the trail.

ACCESSORIES

Having looked at the basics of the mountain bike, I will now consider the add-ons. First I will describe the types of clothing that are available, then turn to the many pieces of essential and optional equipment that you can use to enhance your bike. The aim of this section is to help you make an informed choice before parting with your hard-earned cash.

Clothing

Clothing is easily dismissed as another way of getting fashion-conscious cyclists to part with their money. Most of us started cycling in any old clothes that did the job of keeping us warm and dry. The more time you spend on a bike, however, the more you will find that ordinary clothes can affect enjoyment and even cause discomfort. Some special items are an absolute necessity and should be considered just as essential as the bike itself. The amount and type of riding you do will determine what items you deem dispensable and what are essential. The choice is yours, but before you set off to spend your money, it is worth considering what the various items of special clothing are supposed to do and at what level you are going to be using them.

Getting yourself a good helmet could save your life. Make sure you get one that fits well.

Helmet

The helmet is an essential item. A helmet protects your head in road accidents and is vital when trail riding to prevent injury if you hit a tree branch or go flying over the handlebars.

The inside of the helmet should be lined with a material that will compress and absorb impact; normally this is polystyrene or polypropylene.

Good ventilation is important. The body loses a high percentage of heat through the head and a lot of this heat can be trapped by a helmet. This may not be so much of a problem in the middle of winter, but it could lead to serious heat exhaustion if you are riding for long periods on a hot summer's day.

Replace a helmet as soon as it gets damaged. Do not use a helmet that has been crushed, hit by a hard impact or badly scratched. Even well-looked-after helmets should be replaced after a number of years, whether visibly damaged or not, because the chemical structure of the plastic gradually weakens.

Helmet types

- Hard-shell helmets have a thick exterior shell, usually of plastic. They last longest but are heavy to wear.
- Thin-shell helmets have only a thin outer layer of plastic and are light but expensive.
- No-shell helmets have a soft surface that is easily damaged and so needs more frequent replacement. They are very light. and are available with removable lycra-mesh covers.

Choosing a helmet

Go for a snug fit. The helmet should not move backwards, forwards or sideways when the straps are adjusted correctly. Some helmets can be adjusted internally.

Choose comfort over style. Make sure the helmet does not restrict your hearing and vision. Check that you can fasten and undo the straps easily.

CLOTHING

Helmet standards

Do not buy a helmet that doesn't meet at least one of the following standards:

ANSI Z 90.4 the official US standard.

AS 2063.86 the Australian official standard.

BS 6863: 1989 this British standard is the minimum specification for helmets designed for low-impact use.

SNELL B90 the standard developed by non-profit-making American organisation for high-standard helmets.

Gloves

The main function of gloves is not to keep your hands warm, but to protect them from damage. When you fall off your bike, your natural reaction is to use your hands to break the fall. Bare hands can be badly cut as they are dragged over rough ground.

Strong thick glove palms give the best protection in a fall. Padding in the palm also helps to absorb shock through the handlebar. Fingerless gloves will keep your hands cooler.

Fingerless gloves offer protection from injury and don't interfere with the use of a bike computer.

Insulated gloves reduce feeling and can make the hands too hot. Neoprene gloves will help to keep your hands warm in the wet.

Shoes and socks

The interface between feet and pedals greatly affects comfort and performance. A firm sole is required that doesn't compress and decompress repeatedly, thus wasting energy. Clip-in systems offer a firm base, and once the foot is correctly positioned, it stays there. Because the sole is attached to the pedal any lifting motion acts directly on the pedal. Most clip-in pedals have shoe attachments on both faces of the pedal so that locating the shoe is easier. The system requires special shoes and pedals, and is therefore not cheap. Mountain bike clip-in shoes have the cleat recessed to make walking easier.

Some types of mountain bike terrain are not suited to clip-in shoes. If the terrain involves a lot of walking or carrying, or a lot of mud, then boots and toe clips may be better. Look for boots with a firm sole. Avoid boots with D-rings that catch on the strap, and make sure that boot seams do not catch on the toe straps. Choose a sole pattern that gives grip but will also slide into a pedal easily. Ankle cuffs shouldn't restrict movement but should

Clip-in shoes make more efficient use of your energy. Wool socks are the most comfortable.

consistent comfort level, so there is no one set of clothes that will serve for all weathers.

When you ride a bike your body produces heat and you will sweat. This moisture needs to be transported away from your body if it isn't going to cause discomfort. Some of the moisture will be lost through ventilation and some will pass through clothing. Clothing varies at how well it can do this. Some materials cannot pass the moisture through fast enough before more moisture collects and wets the cloth. The less clothing the moisture has to pass through the better, but wind, rain and cold are all reasons for wearing more or cutting down on ventilation.

The best solution to these problems is provided by the layering system, where each garment performs a different function.

The system comprises three layers, although some garments overlap in their functions, so the number can be reduced to two.

The base layer

Worn next to the skin, this thin layer is designed for comfort; it is usually tight fitting and treated with an antibacterial agent. A properly fitting garment should not restrict movement. Legs and arms should not ride up but they should stay in place when rolled or pushed up. The material should carry moisture away from the body (technically this is known as 'wicking') and provide a measure of insulation. Seams should be flat and smooth: raised seams will chaff against the skin.

The three most popular materials are polyester, polypropylene and chlorofibre. Wool and silk are two other alternatives. Polyester repels water well but needs to be treated chemically to improve wicking. It can be washed and dried at high temperatures without shrinking.

still give support. Boots made of Goretex or similar materials will help to keep your feet dry, but they will not stop water coming in over the top of the boot, so you may want to use gaiters in very wet conditions. Neoprene overshoes will also help to keep your feet dry.

Socks can make a big difference to comfort. Socks made of wool or wool mixtures are best. Avoid cotton in all but the driest conditions. Cotton is good at absorbing water, whether it comes from sweat or elsewhere, but not so good at drying out. If wet cotton rubs against your skin, it can create sore patches that soon become blisters.

Clothing

How wet and cold or hot and clammy you get when cycling will depend greatly on the clothes you wear. Unfortunately, varying conditions require different clothing to maintain a

Dressed for the trail, this rider wears a jacket to keep the wind and rain at bay and leggings to protect the legs.

Polypropylene is very light and thin and doesn't absorb moisture. Chlorofibre boasts a high wick rate, no water absorption and high insulation, but it is prone to shrinking.

Wool is warm even when wet. It takes longer to dry and needs careful washing and drying. Silk feels good, but this, too, needs special care when washing and drying.

Cotton should be avoided at all cost because it is hopeless at transferring moisture and soon becomes waterlogged. Unlike wool, which remains warm when wet because the fibres stay separate, keeping warm air trapped between them, cotton quickly chills and it takes a lot of body heat to dry it out. In a layering system, cotton is a liability because it will cause other layers to become wet, preventing the efficient working of the entire system. While this is widely recognised, the faithful old cotton underpants are often overlooked when preparing for a ride.

Base-layer garments come with a variety of neck designs and sleeve lengths. Some also have zip-up tops and legs.

The mid layer

The mid layer can consist of one or more garments. The aim is to provide sufficient insulation to keep warm while allowing moisture to pass through. Air trapped in the material provides the insulation. While fleece has come to dominate, wool, down and synthetic insulation can also be used. Early fleeces provided little protection from the wind. Advances in the material mean that wind and showerproof garments made of fleece are now available, making it possible to dispense with the top layer.

The top layer

The job of the top layer is to keep wind and rain at bay while not interfering with the functions of the mid and base layer. There are two

The three layer system ensures comfort, insulation, and protection from the wind and wet.

choices in top layers: cheap, light and compact windproofs or more bulky and expensive waterproofs. Both need to be made of materials that can breathe. Waterproof jackets will normally have taped seams, which is a good way of spotting the difference.

Pertex is often used in windproofs and, when treated, can be waterproof to a degree. Waterproofs vary in performance, even between similar materials. The problem is not one of keeping water out, but one of stopping condensation forming on the inside and wetting the mid and base layers.

One common method of waterproofing is to apply polyurethane, or a similar material, to the base fabric. All such coated materials are prone to condensation to a greater or lesser degree. Laminated garments use a membrane between two protective materials. Laminates work better than most coated fabrics, but they cost more. Unless you are going to spend long periods of high exertion on a bike, you may find it difficult to justify buying the most expensive garments.

Leggings

You can apply the layering system to leg wear, but wearing too many layers on the legs will restrict their movement and create a huge heat build up. Wearing shorts off road means that your legs will cut to pieces, even by the mildest looking pieces of vegetation. Bib shorts and leggings provide protection from the cold, but they are not everybody's favourite. For this reason, most cyclists prefer tracksters, leggings or tights.

Whatever you choose, consider how quickly they are going to dry after getting wet, and how stretchy they are. Zips at the leg bottom will help you get them on and off. Stirups will prevent them riding up your leg. Waterproof leggings are available in Pertex and Goretex. With extensive wear, make sure they do not become too baggy at the ankle, or they will brush against the chain ring. The seat of the pants, shorts or leggings is often padded for extra comfort. Avoid seams that run close to delicate parts of the anatomy.

> ### Goretex
>
> Goretex is the brand name for one of the most popular types of laminated material. It consists of a membrane bonded between two fabric layers. This membrane has millions of microscopic pores allowing for a very high rate of moisture transfer.

Design and fit

When riding on a bike, your arms are extended and your back arched. Clothing therefore needs to be specially cut to prevent the sleeves from riding up, or the base of your back from being exposed. Make sure that the top comes down well over your bottom. Try stretching out with your arms; the cuffs should stay in place and there should not be any tightness under the armpits or around the shoulders. Look out for garments made from lycra, often in conjunction with other materials. Lycra makes a good close-fitting but stretchable cloth.

Pockets should be fairly high up, mainly to prevent the contents from catching on your legs. They also need to be out of the way of rucksacks and waistbands. Pockets or pouches low down on the back can be useful.

The overall cut should be close fitting but not tight. Remember you may sometimes want an extra layer underneath. If the cut is too loose the garment will flap and billow. Drawcords around the neck, waist and hem will help ventilation and cut down on billowing.

When buying fleece garments, check the cuffs. Sometimes these are of a different material and non-fleece cuffs can take longer to dry when wet. The cuffs on top-layer garments give better ventilation control if they are adjustable, so velcro tabs are better than elasticated cuffs.

Zips are rather a good ventilation tool, enabling you to open up if you feel hot. They come on the sides, under the armpits and on the front (either part way or full length). Two-way zips add even greater flexibility.

Some manufactures promote the fact that their fleece garments can be zipped to the inside of top-layer garments. This leaves a gap down the front of your body, under the top layer, that isn't covered by the mid layer. In cold and windy conditions, or when you are travelling very fast into the wind, this cold gap becomes very noticeable. A storm flap covering the pockets and front zips on any top is a worthwhile feature.

Combination garments, with wind liners, and garments made of windproof fleece have blurred the distinction between mid and top layers. If you only wear two layers, though, problems can occur when the windproof fleece gets too warm; if you take it off you lose your wind protection. You can get away without a mid layer and just use a base and top windproof layer, but it does depend on the weather conditions.

Reflective strips attached to clothing are a sensible safety feature to look out for.

> ### Bumbags
>
> A bumbag makes an ideal carrier for spare innertubes, windproofs, food, money and the like. Wide belts can be uncomfortable.

Bike Accessories

Some bike accessories are so important that they should be supplied as standard equipment on bikes, but they aren't. Those that are fitted as standard items are not always the best, and you may prefer something else. This chapter tells you what accessories you need and what to look for when choosing between one type and another.

Handlebar ends

Bar ends come in two main shapes: straight or curved. The short straight type is best if you plan to do a lot of climbing, which involves standing out of the saddle to exert more force. Longer curved sections allow the rider to drop

Handlebars have to carry many accessories, though some can be fitted to the frame.

into a tuck, cutting down wind resistance on long fast downhills. This technique is best performed on good surfaces where unpleasant bumps are not likely to be encountered.

Bar ends are usually clamped to the handlebars, sometimes with a reinforcing end plug to prevent the handlebar itself being crushed. Other bar ends have a wedge expander which needs to be used with care to avoid splitting the handlebar open. Bolt-through bar ends are also available, but they increase the risk of damage to the handlebar.

Trip computers and heart monitors

Bike computers are about the size of a large watch and they fit neatly onto the handlebar, or sometimes onto the stem. All computers

measure speed, distance and time; beyond that, there is a choice of other functions. In the case of the most sophisticated versions you can expect the computer to monitor speed, maximum speed, average speed, trip distance, total distance, cadence (the speed at which the pedals turn), heart rate and altitude. In addition, there will usually be a clock built in, with stopwatch and auto start and stop functions.

These computers are linked to a sensor mounted on the fork which senses a magnet fitted to a spoke. Most have a wire link to the computer, but there are cordless examples. Heart rate is monitored by a sensor fitted to the body. The pedal arm is used to fit sensors for computers that measure cadence.

A good computer will show two or more functions simultaneously – it is annoying to have to press buttons to show more than one function. Make sure that the functions they show together are complementary. The display should be clear, with good-sized, easy-to-read characters that do not blur when the wind is in your face on a rough surface. Controls should be positive and not fiddly to operate if you are wearing gloves.

Altitude computers measure differences in barometric air pressure and need to be calibrated at the start of each day (and during the day, too, since air pressure can rise and fall considerably over the space of a few hours). Altitude sensors usually have a small hole to measure the air pressure, but this also lets in water.

Bike computers generally don't like water, so try to keep them dry.

Mudguards

For those who think mudguards are for wimps, try going out in the wet and see how silly you feel with a muddy, cold back, courtesy of the rear wheel. The front wheel will also attempt to blind you with anything it can pick up off the trail and pebble-dash your face in the process. .

The traditional close-fitting mudguards don't have enough clearance to avoid clogging in muddy conditions. Once clogged they are very difficult to clear.

The answer is a guard with a clearance of around 2 in (5 cm). These tend to be less stable and can deform, sometimes catching on the tyre. The alternative is to fit protection guards to the down tube. These cut down – but do not eliminate – mud and water being thrown up as the front wheel turns.

Mud guards will keep you dry by deflecting the mud that is thrown up on the trail.

Front and rear carriers

For touring you will need to attach bike bags to a carrier mounted on the frame. Not all mountain bikes are fitted with the necessary lugs and forks to which a carrier can be attached, so you may need to fit these as accessories.

The choice of carrier material is either aluminium or steel; nobody has produced any in titanium yet. Aluminium is lighter but is

---

Calibration

When you first set the computer up you will need to know the circumference of the wheel. Measure this by marking the tyre and the point at which it meets the ground. Turn the wheel one revolution and mark the ground again. Use this distance when calibrating the computer. Turn the wheel with your weight on it for extra accuracy.

prone to breaking. When this happens on a heavily laden bike you will wish you had chosen the heavier steel.

Large rear panniers benefit from a carrier with a dog-leg design to prevent the bags from folding around and catching the wheel or gears.

Choose bike bags that aren't too long for better ground clearance. Make sure they fit securely to the frame; some have a mechanism to lock them onto the carrier. Cycle bags that convert to a rucksack are handy for when you have to carry the bike, or leave it behind.

Regardless of the claims of the bag manufactures, always treat the bags as not being waterproof and line them with a plastic bag.

Panniers that convert to backpacks are very versatile. Good carriers will stop panniers catching on the wheel.

Handlebar bags

Mounted on the handlebars, bar bags are a convenient form of storage for lighter items. Some come with a shoulder strap and others have an optional camera pocket kit that provides padding for cameras and lenses.

Pack everything securely and make sure the bags don't flap around. A heavily laden bike handles very differently. Fast downhills become a very different experience when the bike bags start swaying around, taking the bike on a different line from the one you want.

Lights

A new dimension opens up when you start riding off road at night. If you don't know why people are frightened of the dark, then you've never ridden a mountain bike at night without lights. Even riding at a sedate 20mph in the dark with a good set of lights feels more like speeding along at 50 mph.

When choosing lights, make sure they meet the legal standard required for road use. Removing your reflectors may be a sorely tempting method of saving weight, but it may not be such a good idea if you get stopped by the police, or if you are involved in an accident. Flashing rear lights, beam patterns and side visibility are all reasons why off-road lights may not be legal for street use.

Rear lights serve only to make you visible to people behind. If they flash, check that they can easily be switched between flashing and constant modes so that they can be used for both and off-road riding. They are not all waterproof, so remember to keep checking them on a wet night, and keep them clean: nobody can see a light caked in mud.

Front lights range in power from under 2 watts to over 35 watts. Urban riding will require a less powerful light compared with off-road riding. Look for powerful lights that have low switches, enabling them to be used for street riding and conserving batteries.

Riding at night is a thrilling experience, but you need powerful lights and absolute concentration.

Some lights have adjustable beams, enabling the light beam to be switched from a broad pattern to a spotlight. It is well worth investing in a battery recharging kit. Rechargable batteries may be more expensive to start with, but they are far cheaper to run in the long term. The batteries are often housed in a bottle cage on the frame. The nuts and bolts securing the cage to the frame can easily shake loose, so check them regularly and carry a few spares.

Bottles and camelbacks

Bicycle frames come with one or two bottle-fixing points. Bottle cages can also be used for holding batteries and tool containers. Camelback water carriers are useful for racing because they do not require the rider to reach down into the frame to get the bottle.

Pumps

Bike pumps are very simple, but there are design differences that will affect their use. The longer the pump the more air will be pumped on each stroke. The same applies to the larger diameter pumps. The larger volume pumps require fewer strokes to inflate a tyre, but more effort at the end of each stroke. There are also double-action pumps that inflate the tube on both strokes of the pump. If you are trying to save weight you may prefer a mini pump, despite its slower rate. Of course your expensive pump will soon get lost, while your cheap pump will survive for years.

The pump can be fitted to the frame by straps, clips or by wedging it inside the frame around the pump mouldings.

Puncture-repair kits

Buy kits that have patches with chamfered (also known as feathered) edges. These blend into the tube and are far less likely to lift or leak at the edges. Keep your eyes open for self adhesive patches. These are a recent development and save carrying tubes of glue.

First-aid kit

Sooner or later you or a trail mate will take a tumble that requires more than a bit of grinning and bearing. First-aid kits can be bought over the counter, but many are bulky, or else so small as to be barely adequate.

If you make up your own kit, the absolute minimum you would need are plasters for minor cuts, antiseptic wipes for cleaning hands and injuries, antiseptic cream for cuts and abrasions, gauze bandage and a small pair of scissors. On longer trips, or where there may be specific local hazards from the fauna or wildlife, extra precautions should be considered.

Just as important as carrying a first-aid kit is knowing how to use it, so consider taking a first-aid course.

Remember, too, that your tetanus jabs should be kept up to date.

After any tumble that lands you in water, such as a canal or river, you should ask your doctor for a check-up for Weil's disease. This is carried in rat's urine and so could be picked up anywhere.

Back every eventuality by carrying a spare inner tube, a puncture-repair kit and a torch if you ride at night.

Locks and security

No matter what you do to protect your bike, thieves will steal it if they have the time and the equipment. You just have to make it as hard as possible for them, remembering that theft is not just a problem that occurs in towns and cities: it also happens out on the trail or while the bike is being transported.

On the trail you should be able to keep your eyes on the bike most of the time. If you can't, then remove one or both wheels and take them with you. Carry a light chain and lock. These measures are often sufficient to deter the casual thief.

Heavier locks and chains are more effective but more cumbersome. Lighter D-locks are popular, and although not impregnable to theft, they offer some of the best protection.

If a thief cannot get the whole bike, they will often settle for the wheels and seatpost, especially if they are easy to remove, courtesy of quick-release bolts. If you use a bike in a high-risk area, consider changing them for more secure bolts.

It does not cost very much to have your cycle marked with a postcode or other mark. This can be carried out by bike shops and is useful for helping the police to trace the rightful owner. When a thief is caught, several bikes are invariably recovered, but often there is no way of identifying the true owner.

It is a good idea to take a picture of your bike and make sure you have an accurate description of it, as well making a record of the frame number. If you haven't already done so, get your bike insured.

Car carriers

There are several types of rack that can be used for transporting your bike by car.

Roof racks are commonly used, but you need a special fitting for each bike. The main disadvantage is that it is often difficult to load

Wise mountain bikers carry a basic tool kit (see page 118) and a first-aid kit when they head for the wild.

Bells and horns

There are some neat little bells on the market that will enable you to warn people of your approach. Try to choose a tone that rings a polite but audible warning, rather than a noise that signals to all and sundry that a mad mountain biker is approaching and that anybody in the way risks death or dismemberment.

a muddy bike onto a roofrack, and you can easily damage the car if the bike drops or slips while loading.

Boot or tailgate racks make use of straps to position the rack. They will carry two, or sometimes three, bikes. They can be fiddly to set up. The strap tension needs to be checked regularly.

Tow-bar racks are a more secure form of fitting. Provided that your car already has a tow bar, they are easy to fit and remove. They will also carry several bikes, depending on the specific rack design. When using tow-bar racks, light boards should be attached to the rear

bike, not only to meet legal lighting requirements but also to let other road users know that you are there and what you are doing.

Protecting paint work

Wrap pipe insulation material, which can be bought from DIY shops and builders merchants, around the tubes and stays of the bike. This makes ideal protection against the risk of paintwork scratches on your bikes and car.

Bike carrying cases

If you are travelling with your bike on buses, trains or aeroplanes, you might want the extra security and protection that a purpose-built bike bag offers. Look for bags made from heavy-duty material with webbing edges to protect the bag from wear and tear. You also want an easy-to-clean and quick drying design. Reinforced bases help to prevent chainring damage. Look for internal wheel straps and padding, and pouches for tools and pedals. Robust, two-way lockable zips are best. Good bags have detachable shoulder straps and carrying handles low down on the side, to allow the bag to be carried under your arm.

Carrying cases are very useful for longer trips – by aeroplane, for example – when you need to dismantle and protect the bike.

(LEFT) Boot racks are an increasingly popular method of transporting bikes to and from the trail.

RIDER PERFORMANCE

Two things affect how well you perform on a bike: fitness and nutrition. This section addresses the questions of how to get fit and stay fit through appropriate training methods. It also looks at the best kinds of food for your regular day-to-day diet, and whilst on the trail.

Fitness

Fitness is a relative concept – different degrees of fitness are needed to undertake different tasks. What matters is whether you achieve the level of fitness that will let you get the enjoyment out of mountain biking that you want. This is an entirely personal thing, but if you find that you tire easily, or cannot perform as you would like, then it is time to look at your fitness. If you are planning a long-distance tour or competitive riding, then it would be foolish to do so without making sure your body is up to it.

Am I fit to train?

Training should only be undertaken if you are healthy and have no medical problems. If you have any doubts whatsoever then consult your doctor.

The BORG scale

Taking pulses and working out percentage heart rates may seem like a lot of trouble. A simpler method is to use the BORG scale of

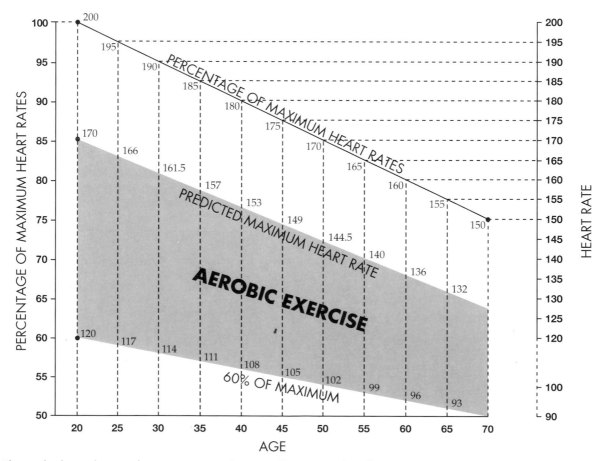

This scale shows that aerobic exercise can dramatically improve the efficiency of your cardiovascular system.

perceived exertion. This well-established system allows riders to judge work rates for themselves simply by assessing how they feel during a particular level of exercise. This is a very good method of controlling what you are doing once you've got the hang of it.

BORG Scale

1. You feel that nothing you are doing is increasing your breathing rate. You could be freewheeling along.

2. You are still doing nothing to increase your breathing. You are probably turning the pedals with little effort over easy ground.

3. You are putting a little more effort in now and there is an increase in your breathing rate.

4. You breathing has further increased as increased effort is needed to maintain speed over more-demanding ground. You are feeling warmer.

5. The ground is more demanding and more effort is needed to keep cadence up (i.e. the speed at which you turn the pedals). Your breathing varies from easy to a fair bit of effort. You are getting warmer and are showing the first signs of sweat.

6. You make an effort to increase speed, your breathing deepens, you get warmer and you are now sweating. There is no muscle discomfort yet. It is still possible to talk.

7. Your muscles can now be felt. You feel good with the effort and feel strong enough to continue.

8. Your thigh and gluteal muscles are starting to feel the effort. Breathing is still controlled. More effort is required to talk and stringing several words together is difficult. You would welcome a slackening of pace.

9. You feel slight burning in the throat and lungs. Your muscles are starting to hurt. Words are single and gasped. You cannot maintain this rate for much longer.

10. You can't go much further. You will have to stop very shortly. Cramp feels it is about to take over from the unbearable pain in your muscles. You cannot talk at all.

Basic training – a step-by-step programme

To see how the BORG scale works in practice, we will now look at a basic fitness training programme. Stage 1 assumes that you are starting from scratch and is designed to tone up your cardiovascular system. If you are already reasonably fit, you could skip stage 1 and proceed straight to stage 2.

Stage 1

To achieve a basic level of fitness you should aim to be taking your bike for a low intensity ride of between 40 and 60 minutes duration, two or three times a week. The objective is to get fit enough to undertake the ride without exceeding seven on the BORG scale – if you can do it at five on the scale, all the better.

Building up to this point of fitness may take several weeks – even several months. Be patient, and use your common sense. Do not do so much that the strain becomes uncomfortable: aches and pains can be a sign that you are overdoing things, rather than that the exercise is doing you good.

Stage 2

The next stage is to improve your aerobic fitness – that is, to ensure that the cardiovascular system is capable of supplying sufficient oxygen to the muscles that they can burn fat. If the cardiovascular system isn't ready for this, the low supply of oxygen will mean that you will start using glycogen stores in the muscles and pretty soon you will feel the pain from the resulting lactic acid build up.

Improving aerobic capacity will, in time, increase the capacity of the heart chambers so that every beat will pump more blood. Your muscles will develop more blood vessels and become more efficient in their use of oxygen. Increased oxygen-carrying heamaglobin blood cells are produced. The net result will be that the heart does not have to work so hard when relaxed, which is why your heart rate goes down when you are at rest.

To increase aerobic performance we now need to increase the heart rate to 70 to 85 per cent of its maximum capability. This represents seven to nine on the BORG scale (see chart on page 73). You should do this by introducing new elements into your riding routine over a couple of weeks, avoiding a sudden leap from one level of training to the next.

Aim to get to the point where you are riding hard at least twice a week. Spend the first 15 minutes getting warmed up, then start to increase the work rate. Ride as hard as you can, approaching nine on the BORG scale (or 85 per cent heart rate) for three to four minutes, or slightly less if you are not yet fully up to it.

After this hard blast, slow down for a while, but don't drop below seven on the scale. When you have recovered, go on another hard ride for another three to four minutes. Two blasts like that should be adequate for each ride. Work towards a fourminute blast, raising the increments slightly and making sure you are fully recovered before tackling the next one, which will probably take 10 minutes.

At the end of the ride, don't just stop – spend the last 10 or 15 minutes warming down. This allows your body time to recover more quickly, before your cardiovascular system slows down.

You will start to notice the difference in fitness after a few weeks. Now when you go out on a recreational ride you will not only be fitter but you will also have learnt a bit about pacing yourself, taking in energy, and controlling your work rate. After each hard ride make the next one a recovery session: that is, go back to the initial stage 1 cardiovascular training sessions, aiming for a 60 per cent heart rate, or six to seven on the BORG scale.

Stage 3

Although your endurance has now increased, you may still find that it is not long before lactic acid starts to burn on some of the more demanding sections. To improve this, you should aim to ride at your limit for six to eight minutes at 85 to 90 per cent heart rate, or eight to nine on the BORG scale. Continue riding after each burst at a slower rate for eight minutes until you recover, then have another go. When you can do this comfortably twice in a session, build each burst up to ten minutes.

Once you start exercising at this rate, you will need to train three or four times a week, including recovery sessions, in order to maintain peak fitness. This begs the question of how much time you can afford to give to maintaining fitness. Everyone's answer will be different. The aim is to reach the level of fitness that you are happy with, then experiment with how frequently and how hard you need to train to maintain that level.

Muscle power

Once you have reached your desired level of cardiovascular fitness, it is time to consider increasing the strength or power of your muscles. To do this, you should ride up a long and gently climbing hill in a fairly high gear, aiming for a cadence of about 60 rpm (cadence is the speed at which the pedals turn – some bike computers will measure this and display the rate). Try this for 30 to 40 seconds. The higher the gear you select, and the slower the cadence, the shorter the time you should cycle for. Take three minutes to recover at an easy pace and then repeat the exercise. Aim to repeat the climb eight times at 30 seconds each, or six times at 40 seconds.

Whilst climbing, concentrate on straightening the leg and forcing the pedal forward. Don't overdo this: you should be aiming for around three to four on the BORG scale. If your muscles feel stiff and sore the following day, you have overdone it – in which case, make the next ride a gentle recovery session. Don't try going through the pain barrier with this one. Eat more protein when you undertake this strengthening exercise: it will be needed to build muscle tissue.

If you are training in preparation for a tour, remember that you will be carrying a lot more weight. Try introducing panniers and rucksacks to the training, beginning with the lower intensity rides. On faster rides start off using low weights and gradually build them up.

(RIGHT) Fitness and muscle power combined will improve your overall stamina and efficiency.

Physical exercise

Stretching exercises should be practiced regularly as part of your training regime. It is a good idea to go through a stretching routine before every ride, to help you warm up, and after every ride, to help recovery. This will also aid your posture and help prevent injury. You may also want to improve your muscle tone by doing the simple stretching and strengthening exercises as described below.

Hamstring

Stand with your feet together. Cross one foot over the other. Bend forward from the hips. Let your head and arms drop into a comfortable position. Hold for 30 seconds. Repeat with the other leg crossed.

Calf

Stand with your feet about two feet from a wall, sufficient that you do not need to stretch forward when you put both hands flat against the wall. Move forward on one foot while keeping the other foot in place. This will stretch the calf muscle. Hold for 30 seconds and repeat with other leg.

Thigh

Stand on one leg. Hold the other leg at the ankle and pull it up, keeping both thighs in line. Keep your back straight. Hold for 30 seconds and repeat on other leg.

Calf raise

Strong calves are needed for pedal power and for walking with your bike. Do this muscle-strengthening exercise on the first step of the stairs. Stand with the balls of your feet on the edge of the step. Your heels should be hanging over the edge. Keep your body straight as you bend your knees. Lower yourself until the calves are tight.

Press-ups

On a bike, your arms and upper body adopt a similar position to the press up. This exercise will help the muscles in your upper body. Put your hands on the floor, with your feet together. Your arms should be straight and parallel, at 90 degrees to your body. Keeping your body straight, lower your chest until it is 2 in (5 cm) off the floor. Hold for a second. Straighten your arms.

Women can vary this exercise by resting on their knees instead of their feet. If this is still too much, bring the knees up more.

Abdomen

By developing the abdominal muscles you take some of the strain off your back. Lie on your back. Cross your arms and place your hands on your shoulders. Bend your knees to 90 degrees. Lift your head and curl your shoulders forward as far as you can without lifting your torso off the floor. Hold for a second. Lower your shoulders slowly.

Back

Back muscles are often neglected. These exercises will strengthen them. Put your hands and knees on the floor. Drop your head between your arms and arch your back upwards. Hold for eight seconds. Raise your head and reverse the back arch. Hold for eight seconds.

Dorsal lift

Lie face down on the floor. Grip your hands together under your chin. Raise your arms and feet, keeping your legs as straight and as high as you can. Hold for twelve seconds.

Suggested exercise routine

In an ideal world, we would all have personal fitness trainers to tailor an exercise programme to our needs. Failing that, you can use the table on the opposite page. This shows a simple programme that will suit most people and, if followed regularly, will help you maintain your muscle tone. To follow the programme, simply repeat each of the exercises the recommended number of times. Warm up beforehand by doing some simple stretching exercises. For consistent results try this twice a week. Don't overdo it by trying to increase the recommended number of repetitions.

Exercise Chart

Exercise	Weeks 1-4	Weeks 5-8	Weeks 9-12
Calf	12	12	18
Thigh	15	15	20
Press-up (men)	8	8	12
Press-up (women)	6	6	10
Abdomen	12	12	15
Back extension	8	8	12
Dorsal lift	8	8	12

Go through the exercises the recommended number of times. In weeks 1-4 aim to repeat the complete sequence three times. Repeat the sequence four times in weeks 5-8. From week 9 the exercises increase in number, but go back to repeating the sequence three times.

 Nutrition

Fatigue and tiredness can set in at any time – on short rides or in the middle of a race. This happens to us all, regardless of our fitness level or strength. We know we are fit enough but we just run out of steam. Why do we run out of steam? What happens in the body that makes us so tired?

Physically demanding activities, such as cycling, use up high levels of energy and water. Food and drink is the fuel that keeps us going, but some kinds of fuel are better than others. In this chapter we will look at each of the three main sources of energy (aerobic, anaerobic and creatine phosphate) and look at how best to fuel them, depending on the level of exertion required, and the efficiency of the muscle.

Aerobic energy

Aerobic energy is produced from oxygen, along with small amounts of blood glucose and free fatty acids. Water, heat and carbon dioxide are produced as byproducts without causing much fatigue. So long as fluid and glucose levels are maintained, and the work rate is within your aerobic resources, then this form of energy will enable you to maintain sufficient stamina to continue riding for extensive periods.

Anaerobic energy

When the effort required increases – say on a hill – the muscle is unable to process oxygen fast enough to burn the free fatty acids. The muscle then has to draw on glycogen (a simple chain of glucose molecules stored within the muscle itself, and in the liver) as an energy source. Using glycogen the muscles produce lactic acid. When lactic acid increases faster than the body can remove it, the build up causes pain. Anaerobic energy is used when the effort reaches such a point that no oxygen is being used and glycogen is the sole energy source. Anaerobic effort can only be sustained for short periods – usually little more than two minutes.

Creatine phosphate

The final energy source available to the muscle is the creatine phosphate contained within the muscle cells. This will last for up to ten seconds at the most – often not that long.

This energy source uses more muscle fibres than the other two. Different work rates utilise different types of muscle fibre and not even the fittest of athletes are able to draw upon them all on a single contraction.

Adenosine triphosphate

Regardless of the energy source, the muscle turns it into Adenosine triphosphate, or ATP. This is the chemical that carries energy for the muscles to work.

Increasing your energy capacity

The aim of the fitness programme described on pages 73–7 is to increase your body's efficiency in using the energy sources available to it. By far the best way of doing this is to increase your body's aerobic resources. Anaerobic energy and creatine phosphate are best thought of as reserve energy sources, kept for when the occasion demands an unusual degree of effort.

For normal cycling, the aim is to increase the capacity of the muscles to process oxygen and burn free fatty acids, so that higher effort levels can be achieved before anaerobic activity starts. Anaerobic capacity can be enhanced by increasing the muscle size and efficiency and by improving the ability of the cardiovascular system to transport blood around the body.

You can also extend the availability of this energy source by increasing the amount of glycogen stored in your muscles and liver. Lactic acid disposal can be improved too. Fitter people are also able to activate more muscle fibre each time a muscle contracts.

On the trail, you should aim to keep your exercise rate at the aerobic level, but there will be sections where the terrain demands more and the glycogen stores are called upon. You should not get into full-blown anaerobic exercise except on very few occasions. Most fit riders can maintain from 90 to 180 minutes of fairly arduous riding in this way, so long as they pace themselves sensibly. When you start to feel the pain of the lactic-acid build up, ease of and allow the body to recover through a period of less-demanding aerobic activity.

By taking in carbohydrates along the way you can further extend your range and make the ride more comfortable. Carbohydrate drinks or energy bars can be used, but chocolate bars and sugar-loaded drinks should be avoided. Most people choose liquid carbohydrates because they are easier to take in and because they also help to replace the water lost through perspiration. Start taking in liquid after about half an hour. If you wait until you are thirsty, your body will already have started to underperform.

Dizziness and blurred vision

Dizziness or blurred vision can result from low blood-sugar levels or from dehydration. When it happens it is essential to stop and take in liquid carbohydrate. Full recovery will take some time, but if you do not stop you are in danger of collapsing altogether. If the symptoms persist, seek medical advice.

Carbohydrates

The amount of carbohydrates you require will vary according to the difficulty of the ride and your size and weight, but a person weighing 70kg (154lb) will typically use between 650 and 750 calories an hour at a moderate to hard rate, and this fuel needs replacing with easily assimilated glucose or glycogen.

Carbohydrates, the best source of glucose or glycogen, are found in vegetables, potatoes, fruit (especially bananas), pulses, nuts, bread (especially wholemeal), pasta, cereals and rice.

Carbo loading

In the build up to a race or a demanding ride you can increase your stores of glycogen by loading your body with carbohydrates for three or four days beforehand. If your training cycle is less demanding in the run up, don't overdo the carbohydrates: the excess will be stored as body fat.

Three hours before an arduous ride you should eat a high carbohydrate meal, but you should eat nothing for two hours before the start. If you ride with large amounts of food in your stomach you will feel sick, because the digestion process is starved of the blood that the rest of the body requires for work.

Eating healthily

The ratio of carbohydrate to fat and protein in a healthy diet continues to be the subject of much debate. Most dieticians agree that we eat too much fat and protein. Most of us would benefit from more exercise. Vitamins, minerals and trace elements are available in sufficient amounts in a balanced diet, so supplements are not normally necessary.

RIDING TECHNIQUES

Mountain biking, as the name suggests, is all about getting off the road or cycle track and on to more challenging terrain. Before you do so, however, it is worth learning and practising some techniques that will help you ride in safety and negotiate some of the hazards you will encounter along even the most innocent-looking tracks – obstacles that can easily derail you if you are travelling at speed. This section will help you learn how to control the bike, use your brakes and gears intelligently and think ahead.

Basic Techniques

Learning a few easy techniques will add to the excitement of riding and ensure that you don't spend your time picking yourself off the ground every time you encounter an obstacle. Handling a mountain bike efficiently is all about moving your arms, legs, shoulders, torso and bottom so as to alter the bike's centre of gravity according to the demands of the terrain. Keeping your body position low also keeps the centre of gravity low. This puts the rider more in control because you do not have to move so far to correct mistakes or to alter your centre of gravity. Moving the centre of gravity forwards and backwards changes the balance of weight between the wheels; this increases or decreases the grip of each wheel, and makes it easier or harder to lift the wheel. All this adds up to the fact that you need good co-ordination between your body and your bike to get the best results when tackling off-road terrain.

Before you even start on some of the more testing terrain, however, you must make sure that your bike is working properly; the brakes, tyres and seat all need to be set up correctly, otherwise you will not be fully in control.

Pedalling and cadence

Pedalling, the actual driving force involved in riding a bike, is often overlooked as being too simple a technique to need explanation. Yet there is a big difference between turning the pedals any old how, and using them to get the best use of the energy you put in.

The rate at which the pedals revolve is called cadence, and this has a direct effect on the energy we use.

For the most efficient use of energy you should aim for a constant cadence of between 70 and 80 revolutions per minute. Between these speeds you will be exercising aerobically and making the best use of your energy reserves. To maintain this rate on different terrain means making intelligent use of your gears. Too high a cadence rate wastes energy and is unproductive. On the other hand, you need to keep dropping down through the gears as the gradient increases. Once you let the cadence drop below 60rpm, greater muscle strength is needed to drive round the pedals. Your muscles will start to exercise anaerobically and you will tire more quickly.

Using straps or clip-in pedals allows you to direct your energy on both the down stroke and the up stroke of the pedal motion. Just lifting the weight of your legs off the pedal on the up stroke makes a difference. With straps or clips you are able to put in some lift and add to the energy transmitted through the drive train.

Downhill riding

Confidence is the single biggest factor in getting the best out of downhill riding. Don't confuse confidence and cockiness, however. You must remain in control of the bike, and be able to stop when you want to, and turn the way you want to go.

The tyre pressures should be set at about 35 to 45psi. Lowering the pressure in this way increases the amount of tyre surface in touch with the ground, thus increasing grip. Lower the saddle so that your bottom can slide on and off the back easily. On steep descents, consider raising the handlebar to shift your centre of gravity to the back wheel and to give you a bit more control.

As a slope steepens, so you need to push yourself further back off the seat, extending your arms. As you move forward again, you will take your weight off the front wheel and lose out on steering control. On the steepest

On downhill runs, let the bike float up and down, absorbing shocks, while you maintain your position.

slopes you may have to hang back so far on the bike that your stomach will be lying on the saddle. Keep your feet level and your arms and legs slightly bent to make the ride more comfortable and give more responsive handling. Let the bike float between you and the ground using the bike as a shock absorber, while keeping your body in the same position.

When you enter a steep slope from the level, the natural reaction is to go over as slowly as possible, and to move back on the saddle in anticipation. Try to avoid this or you will loose balance and steering; keep your speed up as you go over the edge, and wait until the front wheel goes over before moving back in the saddle (see page 91 for more on the techniques of entering drop-offs).

Looking ahead and braking

Your head should always be looking up in the direction you are going, your eyes seeking out a line and recognizing hazards in advance so that they can be avoided.

Braking on a downhill run is intended to control your speed, not to stop you – in other words, you want to brake without the wheels locking up. For best braking control, cover the brake levers with your two inside fingers, pulling the slack out of the cable. In this way you will have immediate and total control over your brakes.

The front brake becomes very sensitive if there is more weight over the front wheel. Getting the balance right takes a little practice but is essential for safe riding – if the front wheel locks or slows too much you will, almost certainly, find yourself crashing over the handlebars.

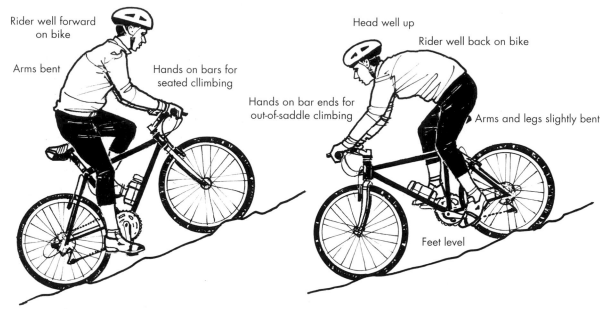

| CORRECT POSITION FOR CLIMBING | CORRECT POSITION FOR RIDING DOWNHILL |

Labels (left illustration): Rider well forward on bike · Arms bent · Hands on bars for seated cllimbing

Labels (right illustration): Head well up · Rider well back on bike · Hands on bar ends for out-of-saddle climbing · Arms and legs slightly bent · Feet level

The rear brake becomes less effective when the balance between braking and skidding gets closer. Moving your weight back over the rear wheel will help restore control. If the back wheel skids, the brakes are no longer effective, so ease off the brakes and push even more weight to the rear of the bike. If you don't, the back wheel will slide to one side.

When both wheels lock, as they most surely will sooner or later, release the brakes immediately and then reapply them, trying to avoid locking up again.

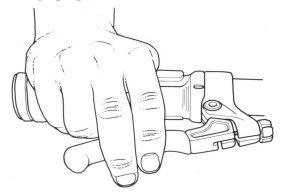

Covering the brakes with the index and middle fingers is a way of taking up slack in the brake cable and increasing the speed of your response. Use the other two fingers and your thumb for grip (see page 83).

Unless you have access to an area specifically designed for the purpose, avoid deliberate skids, even for practising skid control. Skidding for kicks is discourteous to other trail users and gives mountain bikers a bad name.

Climbing

Flying downhill at astronomical speeds is the fun part of mountain biking. Unfortunately, until all hills are equipped with chairlifts, you will have to ride back uphill at some time.

Getting to the top of a steep hill is not just a case of fitness and strength. Technique is just as important too. After a long tiring ride this is even more true. Two things are likely to stop you on your ride to the top: loss of traction and obstacles.

To maintain good traction, or grip, and to help you over humps and bumps, you need to shift your centre of gravity and control your balance at the same time. This is fairly simple at high speeds but managing it at slow speeds, without falling off, is more difficult.

Having said that, it is really quiet easy to develop the correct technique. Experiment on a wide open slope, where you have plenty of room. Remember that the aim is to maintain traction and get over bumps. The more weight you put over the back wheel the more you increase traction. If you go too far back, however, the front wheel lifts off the ground, so the difficult part is controlling the front wheel as it lifts over bumps at the same time as maintaining control over the steering and keeping enough traction going to drive you forward.

The stance you adopt to move your body is important. Sitting and sliding backwards and forwards along the saddle is more efficient than moving your body from a standing position.

Getting uphill without stalling involves selecting the right gear in advance, and maintaining momentum.

Selecting the right gear

When you approach a hill, shift down into the gear you think will be right for the slope and keep in it. Choose one than allows you to hit the slope with your legs spinning and err on the side of a lower gear rather than a higher one, because changing gear on the hill will interrupt your flow and rhythm. As the slope steepens you will need to ease your body forward to keep the front wheel on the ground. A momentary lessening of rear-wheel traction may be necessary if this is the only way to keep the bike going in the direction you want. As soon as you are on line, ease your weight to the back again.

Obstacles

When you meet an obstacle, move back on the bike, taking the weight off the front wheel, and pull a gentle wheelie. Move forward as the front wheel rolls over the obstacle, taking weight off the rear wheel so that it can roll over too. With practice you will soon be able to lift the rear wheel over any obstacle, thus cutting down the chances of it stopping you.

Maintaining momentum

Start using your arms as the slope gets harder, pulling forward on each pedal stroke; not only will this keep you peddling, it will also help keep the front wheel on the ground.

If you are losing power you may have to stand out of the saddle to avoid changing gear. On a poor surface be careful that you don't move your weight forward at the same time and lose grip.

Using the handlebars

Your use of the handlebar ends will differ, depending on whether you are sitting or standing. Using the handlebar itself while sitting ensures that your hands stay close to the brakes for a quick and controlled dismount. By contrast, using the bar ends while seated will let you pull yourself further forward.

In the standing position the bar ends let you get further forward still, adding stability, because your arms are further apart, and allowing you to sway the bike from side to side to give you more power.

Looking ahead

Picking a line whilst going uphill is just as important as on a downhill run. Follow the line that offers the best traction and least resistance. Loose gravel and wet grass should be avoided, though there will come a time when you've got to deal with them. When this times comes, try to keep as straight a line as possible, because sudden turns will probably turn into a skid.

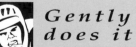 **Gently does it**
As you adjust your stance and alter your technique, do it gently. The smoother your actions, the more efficient you will be and the less likely you are to induce a mishap.

As you get tighter into the bend, lean over and drop your outside foot.

Cornering

Improving your cornering technique will give you the confidence to take bends faster. Conversely, you could end up with some grazes, or even broken bones, if you don't master these skills. The point of fast cornering is to maintain your speed for the obstacles and hills that lie around the bend.

There are three points to remember when taking corners: they are line, control and position. All three are affected by the track's surface and width. On narrow tracks there might

only be one line. Rutted or well-worn parallel tracks may offer a limited choice, even on some of the wider tracks.

Line

Choosing the right line gets easier with practice, though you may have to allow for rocks or holes. Keep in as straight a line as possible, coming into the bend on the outside, aiming for the apex of the bend on the inside, then heading towards the outside of the bend again

The key technique for tackling mud is to select the right gear, and keep moving.

as you straighten up and exit from the curve. It may be difficult to judge where the apex is on an unknown bend and a bend that tightens or slackens as it turns will affect your judgement too. If you start to cut across towards the furthest visible point of the inside of the bend, modifying your line if the bend alters in character, you should get close enough to the apex to maintain your balance.

Control

For best control through the corner, you should brake before you start to turn; don't brake in the turn, or you risk losing traction. As you pass through the apex, start to accelerate. If your back end starts to break away, slacken off a little; as long as the rear wheel keeps on turning, this drifting is not likely to turn into a skid.

Position

As you go through the bend your weight needs to shift from side to side; your position may only change a little bit, but unless it does, your line and control techniques are wasted. As you enter the bend keep your feet level. As you get tighter into the bend, lean over more and drop the outside foot, transferring your weight onto it. This will lift you out of the saddle slightly and the saddle will now be touching against the inside of your left leg. Dropping your inside shoulder and knee will also make a difference, but be wary of getting caught in the undergrowth.

As you pass through the apex, prepare to accelerate. Move your shoulder and knee back into place and push down with your inside leg. The bike will flip back upright and, without your noticing, you'll be back in the saddle.

Tackling mud

What do you do when mud comes into the equation and starts mucking up your climbing and cornering technique, or just your efforts to keep going? Tyres make a big difference. Fit tyres with large, well-spaced blocks that allow the mud to be squeezed out. Low tyre pressures also help, by allowing the tyre to flex and dislodge mud better.

In mud the most important consideration is to keep moving. When all else fails, try 'hotching' the bike forward. This technique is quite easy and should be used long before you grind to a sticky halt. On each power stroke you need to push the bike forward under you in what is known as a hotching motion. Before you get into the next pedal stroke, gently move back again ready for the next hotch. The hardest bit is moving gently back without causing the bike to hotch back the way it has just come.

When riding in mud, overgear a little, and select your gear before you enter the hazard. If you enter the mud in too low a gear, the rear wheel is more likely to spin, and forward motion will stop. To get moving again, you should slacken off on the pedals and give an almighty hotch. It is far better, though, to keep the pace smooth and even, thus preventing the risk of wheel spin.

Acrobatics

Once you have mastered the basic techniques, it is time to tackle something more adventurous. You will, no doubt, have noticed that some riders spend a lot of time off the ground, giving a new meaning to the term 'off-road biking'. They always seem to be jumping, hopping or flying over something. It looks flash and it is fun, so don't be a stick in the mud – have a go. In any case, some of those tricks can actually help on awkward trails.

Bunnyhops

Bunnyhopping is a trick associated with BMX riders, and it is perhaps something that you've done without knowing it. Bunnyhopping is lifting the front wheel over an obstacle, and it's a technique well worth mastering.

To lift the front wheel off the ground pull up on the handlebars and pedal very hard. The front wheel should lift. If it doesn't, try again, pulling harder on the handlebars, and remembering that you want upward motion, not forward. With practice you will soon be able to lift the front wheel high enough to enable you to hop up onto pavement kerbs.

Once you can do that, start lifting the back wheel too. This will probably require what feels like a rather awkward lifting and pushing back of the feet.

The next step is to put these two together and practice getting both wheels in the air at the same time. Once you have learned to bunnyhop, you can use the technique when you come across rocks, roots or whatever other obstacle presents itself.

Speed jumps

For some riders, speed jumping comes as a natural extension from the bunnyhop, although it is a different technique. You may even find this easier to do. Start by moving over level ground at slow speed, with plenty of balance. Stand up on the bike, with the pedals level, then crouch down, bending your arms and legs, and jump. Bring the bike up with you as you straighten your arms and legs. Keep your arms and legs slightly bent to absorb the energy as you return to earth.

Bunnyhopping is not just done to look flash – it is a sound technique for getting over obstacles.

Once you have mastered speed jumps you can fly over gullies, potholes and even small streams.

Persevere at this one, as it may not come straight away. At first you may only be able to get one wheel in the air. If so, try altering your balance slightly. You should also make sure the toe straps are tight. Clip-on pedals have a habit of coming undone as your knee twists in the jump.

When you can jump consistently, it is time for the next stage. Adding a bit of speed means that the jumps get longer. Put some small sticks in your path and jump these, steadily building up the size of the jump.

This technique will really improve your riding: no more stopping for channels that cross your path, and no more dropping warily into holes.

Bombholes and drop-offs

Now that you have learnt to fly, let us look at another application for this skill. Your skill in entering drop-offs and exiting from bomb-holes can be greatly improved by the judicious use of a little bit of air time.

A bombhole exit is like a launch ramp. You need to know how to control your take off and landing if you want to avoid a crash landing. Take care not to catch the rear wheel on the lip or you could get kicked over the handlebars. If you put in a bunnyhop just before the top of the ramp and you've got it right you should land on the flat and continue in a forward motion. If you find yourself stopping at the top, try it a bit faster or leave the jump until later. With a bit of practice it should not be long before you get the knack.

The prospect of entering a drop-off at speed may seem a bit more daunting. You need to have perfected a good jump technique before you try this. Think about the way ski-jumpers hit the sloping ground at high speed, using the slope of the ground to maintain their speed. Your task is a lot simpler, but the principal is the same. Practice on a short gentle slope with plenty of run out. As you approach the edge of the drop-off, put in a jump that carries you over the edge, but not too far. Ideally you should land with both wheels on the slope simultaneously. Favour the rear wheel landing first, rather than the front one.

Bike set up

Lower the saddle when you expect to do a lot of jumps. This way you are less likely to be tipped over the handlebars by the seat if you land awkwardly.

Air control

While you are in the air, keep your arms and legs slightly bent to absorb landing impact. If the front wheel looks likely to land first, lean back a little; if the front wheel lands before the rear wheel you will lose control. It is best if both wheels land together, but, if the rear wheel lands first, put in a little dab on the rear brake – this will pull the front wheel down.

Trackstands

This is a method of stopping and maintaining a stationary position without putting your feet down. Learning to do this can save time, eliminating the delay that occurs while you try to put your feet back on the pedals and get moving again.

Start at the bottom of a gentle slope. Choose an easy mid-range gear, not too low. Set off up the hill and slow down to a slow stop. With one pedal crank arm about 30 degrees above the level, turn the front wheel about 45 degrees towards the raised foot. As the bike tries to go back down the hill, apply pressure to the raised pedal without turning it. You may find that a gentle rocking motion helps you to maintain your balance. If you roll too far back, you will not have enough crank

(RIGHT) Sideways hops are good for getting you out of a rut – even if only into another one.

Bottoms up – endo turns let you change direction in mid air using your hips.

leverage to control the bike. If you find you've nearly got it, but you can't get the rocking motion quite right, experiment with different gears. With practice you should be able to hold a still pose without the rocking.

Sideways hops

Once you've conquered the trackstand, and perfected your jump technique, you can have a go at sideways hops. These are very useful for getting out of a rut.

Position yourself at an angle to the line of a gentle slope, and get into a trackstand. Lean up towards the top of the slope and jump. Grip the bike with your thighs and use hip movements to propel the bike sideways and uphill.

Once you can do this, try putting several hops together. Practice hopping in both directions, but always up the slope. In time you can try hopping over small sticks and then build

from there. You may find that, once you have mastered the basic sideways hop, you can improve your technique faster by trying it out on the move.

Endo turns

This type of turn may at first seem completely alien to everything you should do on a bike. You are actually trying to get the rear wheel off the ground, whilst keeping control of the bike. The position will not be new to anybody who has come off over the handlebars (and that probably means most of us). The problem is overcoming the gut reaction that tells us this is all wrong. It is worth persisting, because this technique is very useful on narrow tracks, especially for weaving in and out of trees.

You should practice this without straps or clip-in pedals so as to make dismounting a bit safer. Find a soft level surface and ride slowly. Apply the front brake gently and move your weight forward. You will feel the lifting effect,

even if you don't get the rear wheel off the ground to begin with. Once you start to get a few inches of lift, try holding it for a couple of seconds before letting the rear wheel return gently to the ground. When both wheels are back on the ground, you should be able to hold a trackstand or ride away.

Having achieved this, you can put the turn in. As you lift the back wheel off the ground, turn it in the direction you want to go, but not too far. Use your hips as a pivot to swing the bike around. Be ready to compensate a bit as the rear wheel hits the ground, or you will lose your balance.

At first your turns will be slight, but you will turn further as you learn to keep the rear wheel off the ground for longer. Once you have got this far, practice twisting the bike faster and be prepared to make some decisive turns of the front wheel at the same time, so that you end up pointing in the direction you want to go, and ready to continue riding forward.

Crashing

You don't need teaching how to crash: this is just something that happens from time to time. No matter how good a rider you are, crashes will still happen.

The relief of surviving a crash can be short lived if the bike has been damaged in the process. The aim, therefore, is to live through the excitement and try to do so with an undamaged bike. Here are some damage limitation exercises to consider.

Going over the handlebars is probably the most unnerving method of dismounting. The prospect of your face paying for your errors can work wonders on the adrenalin. The initial response is to let go of the handlebars and use your outstretched arms to break your fall. This should be resisted. Get your feet out of the clips and straps first, then push the back of the bike away from where you are falling. Sometimes you may be lucky enough to land on your feet, but don't count on it – instead, try and aim for a comfortable landing place.

When you do hit the ground try not to let your hands become skids. Even when wearing gloves you risk shredding the palms of your hands. Try and roll to break the fall, though beware of rolling if you are likely to collide with a more dangerous object and cause an even more serious injury, especially to your head.

When the bike slides sideways from under you, try and stay with the bike. Removing your feet from pedals could mean that a pedal buries itself in your leg when you land. Instead you can use your legs to push on the pedals and move the bike away from you, so that any sudden stops don't result in the top tube injuring your groin.

Holding onto the handlebars will help to protect your hands against impaling by bar ends, brake levers and the handlebar itself. By keeping hold of the handlebar you can also keep the front wheel from turning under the bike and causing damage.

Falling off the back of the bike can be really bad news, especially if the bike rears up and lands on top of you. Put your feet on the ground and just let the bike roll away between your legs.

WHERE TO RIDE

The whole point of mountain biking is to get off the tarmac and onto the more challenging terrain of forest paths, canal towpaths, green lanes or even hills and high mountains. Choosing where to practice your sport does depend upon advance planning, however. Not everybody welcomes mountain bikers, and not all land is open to the public. This section looks at the essentials of route planning and navigation, and then runs through the attractions and legalities of riding in various countries.

Route Planning

Before you even set out on an off-road trail, you must find out whether the route is open to mountain bikes. This means learning to read a map and identify suitable public rights of way. Just because a right of way exists, it does not mean that it is open to cyclists.

In national parks, for example, cycling is restricted to certain routes so as not to cause erosion or disrupt walkers. Where routes are open to cyclists, it is important to observe certain standards of behaviour – the actions of a few inconsiderate mountain biker can easily lead to a ban on all cyclists.

There are several different cycling codes of conduct but most have the following elements in common: give way to walkers; approach horses and other animals with care; avoid skids; respect private property; think ahead and be prepared.

Navigation

Where parks cater for mountain bikes, they usually have maps showing the trails that you can use. Routes are often signposted so that you don't get lost. Once you start to explore away from the beaten track, however, it will be necessary to learn how to read a map and interpret various landscape features. Beginners should consider going on one of the navigation courses that are often available through cycling clubs or other outdoor groups. Even if you are competent at using maps on your home territory, remember that the format and accuracy of maps varies greatly from one country to another.

Contours and gradients

Contours are the lines on maps that can tell you a great deal more than just how high the ground is above sea-level. Using your intelligence you can, for example, work out what the weather conditions are likely to be at a given altitude at different times of the year and plan your trip accordingly. Cloud cover is another important consideration, as well as rain, snow, wind, humidity and temperature.

A contour traces a line over the ground at one constant height. Depending on how close the contours appear on the map it is possible to gauge how steep or flat the terrain is. The closer the contours are, the steeper the hill. Widely spaced contours indicate a shallower gradient.

Heights are shown on some of the contour lines, and this can help you work out which way the ground rises or falls, but it can still be confusing. Remember that rivers will always be in the bottom of a valley and that the contour either side will usually mark rising ground. The intervals between contours will vary between maps: some may be 15ft (5m) apart, while others may be as much as 150ft (50m) apart.

Compass points

A compass needle points to magnetic north, which is not located at the true north pole. The variation between magnetic north and true north differs according to where you are on the globe, and the position of magnetic north moves slightly every year. Good maps will indicate the direction and variation so that you can work out precisely where magnetic north is at a given time.

When using a map and compass, it is easy to assume that the grid lines on the map run north to south and east to west. On some maps this is true, but don't take it for granted. The variation is only likely to be slight but it is important to be aware of this and make allowances. Again, a good map will have marginal notes indicating any variance between grid north and magnetic north.

UNDERSTANDING GRID REFERENCES AND CONTOUR LINES

Grid References

To make maps easier to use, most are split into a grid. The Ordnance Survey, for instance, has a grid that covers the entire UK.

Simple, 4-figure grid references are obtained by reading the figures straight off the map. To obtain a reference first read off from the numbers that run horizontally, and then those that run vertically. Use the numbers to the bottom left of the square in which the object being described is placed. For instance the church appearing in the bottom left square would be at reference 3021.

A more precise reference is obtained by mentally sub dividing the square into a hundred smaller squares, as shown by the grey rules. In this case the church is at a position 5 rules in and 4 rules up. The six-figure reference would therefore be 305214.

Contour Lines

Contour lines indicate how high and how steep the terrain is at any point. The more closely spaced they are, the steeper the slope. Thus the north side of this hill has a very sharp drop, while the southwestern slope has a more gentle gradient.

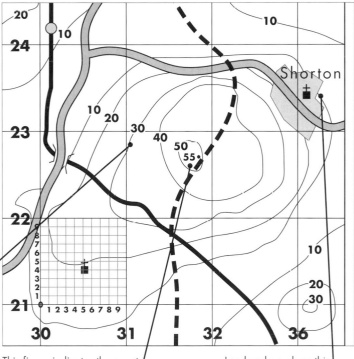

This figure indicates the exact height above sea level. Spot points like this usually indicate the highest point in the immediate vicinity.

Landmarks such as this church are invaluable for checking your location, or working out your location, should you become lost.

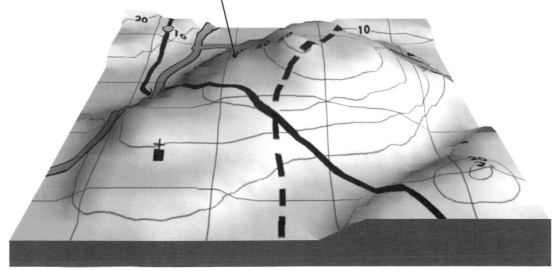

COMPUTER SIMULATION OF CONTOUR LINES

A COMPASS

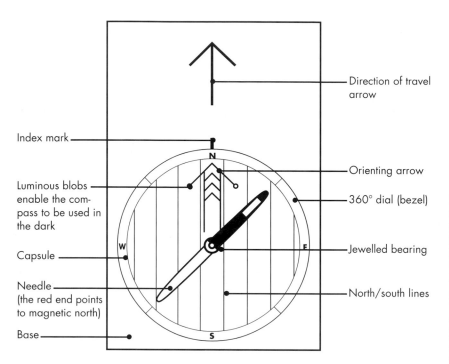

Direction of travel arrow

Index mark

Luminous blobs enable the compass to be used in the dark

Capsule

Needle (the red end points to magnetic north)

Base

Orienting arrow

360° dial (bezel)

Jewelled bearing

North/south lines

VARIATION OF NORTH

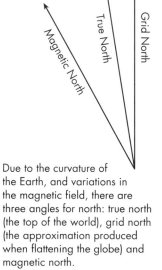

Due to the curvature of the Earth, and variations in the magnetic field, there are three angles for north: true north (the top of the world), grid north (the approximation produced when flattening the globe) and magnetic north.

The differences between the three vary depending on your location. If you require a very accurate reading you may need to take this into account. All Ordnance Survey maps describe this variation for the area projected on the map.

WORKING OUT YOUR LOCATION USING A MAP AND COMPASS

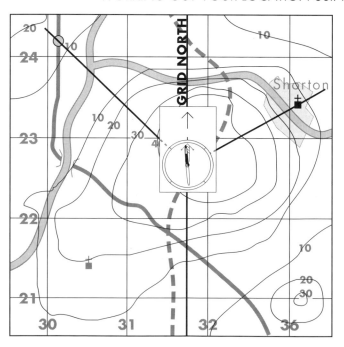

Use your compass to orientate the map correctly so that it is facing north. You should then be able to pick out landmarks to navigate by. Obviously it is easier to do this if you choose a hill or promontory that allows you a clear view of the surrounding countryside. Other tall objects in the landscape, such as church towers and spires, electricity pylons or hilltops are all useful landmarks to check your position by.

Most of the time you will not need to use a compass. The surrounding features on the ground are usually sufficient to enable you to locate your position on the map. Problems arise, however, when tracks appear that are not shown on the map, or more commonly when there is no defined track on the ground, though there is one shown on the map. When this happens, you can use the compass to check on your current location, then keep updating your position with frequent references to the map. Start by lining the map up with north, using your compass and allowing for variations in magnetic and grid north. Look for a landmark and plot its direction using the markings on the compass. Do this with two, or (better still) three, landmarks. Where the lines cross should be your position.

Don't blame the map

Sometimes your brain tells you to disagree with what your map and compass tell you, but thinking the map is wrong, and that you are right, is potentially very dangerous. If you are convinced that things aren't right, check that nothing is affecting the compass. Standing astride a bike while using a compass and expecting the needle to point north ignores the possible magnetic influence of the bike. Bridges, powerlines, pipelines and other steel objects will all influence a compass needle.

Heading off

There comes a time in every cyclist's life when the absence of a track is compounded by the lack of any features to help you navigate across the vast and featureless expanse that must be crossed. This is most likely to happen in the dark, when any landmarks that exist are concealed. Before you set off, it is vital to know where you are. You can then choose a landmark on the map that you are going to head for. The problem here is that, especially in poor visibility, you could pass within feet of the landmark and miss it, no matter how good you are at following a straight line (and most of us are not that good).

The answer is to choose a landmark with a linear feature that runs through it. A bridge over a river is a good example. You want to cross the river but can only do so at the bridge. If you head for the bridge and find a river, but no bridge, you have a problem. You know the bridge is on the river somewhere, but you don't know whether it is to the right or the left. What you do, therefore, is to head off deliberately to one side of the bridge, rather than aiming for the bridge itself. That way, once you reach the river you know in which direction the bridge should be. When deciding which side of the bridge to head for you need to consider the ease of the route and the opportunities for finding other landmarks along the way to check your position against.

This technique can be employed utilising many different features of the landscape, such as roads, hedges, fences and powerlines.

Global positioning systems

Global positioning systems (GPS) have been around for a long time, and are greatly used in yacht navigation. They will pinpoint your position with absolute accuracy, using satellite technology. Hand-held devices, weighing a few pounds, now make them a practical proposition for the adventurous mountain biker, especially if you are planning a trip through poorly mapped regions of the world.

Apart from the initial cost of purchasing a GPS device, the main drawback is its appetite for batteries. If used daily as an hour-by-hour navigation aid, you could run out of juice on a long expedition. GPS devices are best used as a back up for checking your position two or three times a day. They are extremely accurate, so don't dismiss their readings; that is a certain route to getting yourself lost.

⬛ Riding in Different Countries

Mountain biking is a popular sport in many different parts of the world, and there are exciting trails to explore, ranging from the most taxing mountain paths to gentle recreational routes built along defunct railway lines. This chapter can do no more than whet your appetite by describing some of the most popular mountain-biking destinations. More information can be obtained by contacting the various organisations whose addresses are given in the text. Most are bodies set up to represent the interests of cyclists and they will give you advice on the laws and voluntary codes concerning mountain biking in their country or region.

Australia

Such a huge and sparsely populated country as Australia provides a natural environment for the mountain bike. The country has everything, from snow-covered mountains and deserts to rainforests and crocodile-infested waters.

All state forests and national parks have an open-access policy. Maps and route descriptions can be obtained from bike shops and park offices. Walking trails shown on maps are open for bikers to use, but riders must always give way to walkers.

Getting to some of the better trails can be an expedition in itself. If you contact local clubs or bike shops in towns and cities, they can give you tips on how to find some good trails without travelling too far. While doing so, check that you are not breaking any laws

The Three Sisters in the Blue Mountains of New South Wales, Australia.

using your bike in these areas; wilderness areas are protected environments, for example, and mountain biking is prohibited.

Australian Rails for Trails is an organization dedicated to utilizing old railway lines for recreational use. For something more adventurous, the Mawsons Trail will test you to the limit. This old road follows one of the pioneer explorers' trails and runs from South Australia into Central Australia.

Australian Cycling Federation

68, Broadway,
Sydney, NSW 2207
Australia.

Canada

Canada is a country of big wide-open spaces, but that doesn't mean you can cycle wherever you want. Much land is privately owned, and it is best to use designated mountain-bike routes, of which there are many within reach of the major Canadian cities. Provincial Parks also have specified mountain bike trails. Soon it will be possible to cross Canada by bike: the Trans-Canada Trail is an ambitious project designed to create some 6,250 miles (10,000 km) of bike trail. It is due for completion by the year 2000.

Canadian Cyclist Association

1600 Promenade James,
Naismith Drive,
Gloucester,
Ontario K1B 5N4,
Canada.

France

The growth of mountain biking in France has led to the creation of Mountain Bike Centres located throughout the country, from where you can get advice on local routes. The long-distance footpaths that crisscross France are, unless otherwise stated, open to mountain

(LEFT) Exploring the mountains of Alberta in one of Canada's many National Parks.

bikes. In nature reserves there is only limited bike access. The heavy use of mountain bikes in the Fontainbleau Park near Paris has led to strict controls.

Away from the major cities, things are far more relaxed. In ski areas, mountain bikes are often seen as an important source of summer revenue and there are plenty of opportunities for some exciting off-trail biking in the Alps or the Pyrenees, for example.

Federation Français de Cyclisme

Z. A. C. de Nanteuil,
Im. Jean Monnet,
5 Rue de Rome,
F - 93561, Rosny Sur Bois,
France.

Vercors

The Vercors region of France offers some magnificent biking. This is an area of deep gorges that create an impenetratable feel. It is also on the European Bike Express route (a bus service that transports bikes and riders around Europe – see page 112), making this an easy part of France to reach.

Germany

Germany's vast Black Forest region, along with the Hartz mountains and the Bavarian Alps, all cater for mountain biking. Most routes are waymarked, and the 1:50,000 Kompass Wanderkarten maps are very useful for finding your way along remote footpaths and tracks.

Cycling is not allowed on trunk roads, dual carriageways or motorways in Germany. Bikes can be taken on trains that have luggage cars, so long as there is room, but you have to load them yourself.

Bund Deutscher Radfahrer Ev

Ottofleck Schneise 4,
D - 60528, Frankfurt am Main,
Germany.

(PREVIOUS PAGES) Many ski resorts in the Alps offer cut-price accommodation during the summer months. This can be an inexpensive way of exploring some of Europe's most exhilarating landscapes.

Italy

Italy's mountainous terrain and its numerous *strada bianca* (white roads – unsurfaced rural roads used by farmers but open to all vehicles) make this a great country for cycling. Unfortunately, it is difficult to get comprehensive information about mountain biking from one source. Cycle clubs and shops, and alpine clubs, are your best bet for local information.

The mountain-bike section of La Federazione Ciclista Italiana (The Italian Cycling Federation) is currently compiling maps and routes suitable for mountain bikes.

Italian military maps (the equivalent of the Ordnance Survey) are notoriously inaccurate and out of date. There are, however, excellent German maps of several areas of northern Italy (notably the Dolomites, northern Tuscany and Umbria) showing footpaths (where cyclists are tolerated) and white roads.

Federazione Ciclista Italiana

Stadio Olimpico - Curva Nord,
Cancello L - Porta 91,
1-00194, Roma,
Italy.

New Zealand

Mountain biking is widely accepted in New Zealand as an outdoor pursuit. On the other hand, National Parks only allow bikes on maintained roads (which includes unsurfaced maintained roads). The key word here is 'maintained', so if it is an abandoned mining road it is out of bounds to cyclists. Forests and Regional Parks are more receptive and normally make efforts to encourage mountain bikes with waymarked routes and maps.

New Zealand has a fine network of hiking routes, but these are currently closed to mountain bikes. There are some exceptions and the situation is liable to change.

Competitions

The New Zealand Cyclic Saga was inspired by the British Polaris Challenge (see page 112). It combines the physical challenge of mountain biking with the skills of orienteering. The two-day event has a touring category for competitors who want their overnight gear transporting to the campsite. Less demanding is the Karapoti, a 35-mile (56-km) race that takes place near Wellington and attracts over 1,000 entrants. This is followed every summer by the Big Coast event, which attracts 5,000 people for a two-day fun ride around Wellington.

New Zealand Cycling Association

PO Box 45-048,
Christchurch,
New Zealand.

The national body representing all cyclists in New Zealand.

New Zealand Mountain Bike Association

PO Box 361,
Timaru,
New Zealand.

The national body representing mountain bike interests in New Zealand.

South Africa

Political changes mean that it is now easier to travel to and within South Africa, thus opening up a country with a wide diversity of terrains. Getting to South Africa is quite expensive, but travel and accommodation costs can be low once you are there. Fortunately, South Africa has a strong and thriving network of mountain-bike clubs and a good selection of routes.

Nature reserves offer some of the best trails, although you will have to check on the current rules for bikes. Legislation is being considered by the South African government to control vehicle use in the nature reserves, and it is possible that mountain bikes will be treated as any other vehicle, and controlled in the same way.

Outside of the national parks and nature reserves there are several long-distance trails open to cyclists, hikers and horses. Among the best are the Cedara Forest Trail (Hilton, Natal), the Early Settlers' Trail (Gauteng), the Long Tom State Forest Trail (Eastern Transvaal), the Christmas Krans Trail (Orange Free State), the Homtinl Trail (Eastern Cape), the Jonkershoek Nature Reserve (Western Cape) and the Longmore Forest Trail (Port Elizabeth).

SAMBA (South African Mountain Bicycle Association)

PO Box 1227,
Pinetown 3600,
South Africa.

WILD

Women in Love with Dirt (WILD) is a group that encourages women to get involved in mountain biking. They can be contacted through the South African Mountain Bicycle Association.

Spain

Europe's second most mountainous country offers plenty of scope for mountain biking. The paths and tracks of the Spanish countryside have, until relatively recently, served as links between remote mountain villages and they make some of the best riding. The Pyrenean ski resorts offer a rich choice of high-altitude routes, and many will let you take your bike on ski lifts

Most recognized walking routes can be used by mountain bikers, too, though some walking routes involve steps and climbs that may be impassable by bike.

Some Spanish routes are well-known to adventurous cyclists. One is the Cantabrian Cornice, in the northwestern corner of Spain, which is exciting, if windy and wet from Atlantic fronts. The Iberian mountain range offers a wealth of tracks and paths suitable for mountain bikes. Tracing the source of the River Tagus or attempting the peak of San Lorenzo at 7,421ft (2,262m) are two demanding challenges in the range.

The Central Mountain chain has a number of well-signposted routes. In Credos there are two routes of special interest, from Hoyos del Espino and Navarredonda de Gredos. At Navacerrada the ski lift can be used in the summer.

Andalusia has mountains over 9,842 ft (3,000 m) high. There are a wealth of tracks that can be strung together to make good routes. Signposting is not very good, so a decent map is essential.

In addition, some 4,375 miles (7,000 km) of disused railway lines are being converted to green trails in Spain. The Cadiz Mountain Trail is one that runs for 40 miles (65 km).

Federacion Espanola de Ciclisomo

Ferraz 16-5,
E - 28008,
Madrid,
Spain.

United Kingdom

Britain's extensive rights-of-way network allows mountain bikers to pursue their sport with a freedom that is rare in other countries. Even so, it is important to abide by the law, and the law prohibits mountain bikers (and, indeed, all cyclists) from riding their bikes on public footpaths. Cyclists are allowed to use three types of public rights-of-way: bridleways, roads used as public paths (also known as byways open to all traffic), and the public highway.

All these rights-of-way are shown on British Ordnance Survey maps, and each type of right-of-way is designated by a specific symbol. Perhaps of greatest interest to mountain bikers are the unmaintained roads, or byways. If you are in any doubt about the status of any particular route, you are entitled to inspect local Highway Authority maps, which are held at District Council offices, and in some local libraries.

(FOLLOWING PAGES) Following a track through Fantasy Meadow in the Winter Park resort, Colorado, USA.

Another option is to use canal towpaths. To do this, you must first obtain a British Waterways permit (see below for address). These are cheap to buy, are valid for one year and come with a directory listing where you can and cannot ride.

Many local authorities and other voluntary organisations have also devised cycle routes. These range from urban routes designed primarily for commuters, to long-distance routes with the emphasis on scenery and wildlife. A good starting point for information is the local tourist office in any town, many of which stock a comprehensive selection of guides, including cycle routes. Good books and guides are often available at National Park Information Centres.

Polaris Challenge

Britain's Polaris Challenge involves two days of riding a mountain bike over some of the wildest and remotest terrain in Britain while carrying a full complement of camping equipment. Over 1,000 competitors do this twice a year, often facing snow, deep frost and blizzards in the process. In fact, the Polaris Challenge is regarded as one of the hardest mountain-bike events in the world.

British Cycling Federation

National Cycling Centre,
1 Stuart Street,
Manchester
M11 4DQ,
United Kingdom.

The organization that represents mountain bike interests in Great Britain.

British Waterways

Willow Grange,
Church Road,
Watford
WD1 3QA,
United Kingdom.

The body responsible for canal towpaths, among other things. Issues bike permits, without which cyclists may not use towpaths.

Cycle Touring Club (CTC)

69 Meadrow,
Godalming
GU7 3HS,
United Kingdom.

Offers insurance, legal advice and information on cycling in the UK and abroad.

European Bike Express

31 Baker Street,
Middlesborough
TS1 2LF,
United Kingdom.

Every summer this organization runs a bus service that transports bikes and riders through the United Kingdom, France, Spain and Italy. The service operates once or twice a week. CTC members receive a discount.

Sustrans

35 King Street,
Bristol
BSA1 4DZ,
United Kingdom.

This charity works to promote sustainable transport in the United Kingdom. It encourages the use of bicycles and gets involved in projects like the restoration of railway lines for recreational use, and the creation of national bridleway routes that can be used by horse riders and by cyclists.

United States of America

Mountain biking was born in America, and it is not surprising that this vast country has some of the best mountain-bike terrain to be found anywhere. The Bureau of Land Management, the US Forestry Service and the National Parks Service all manage massive amounts of public land, threaded by a network of trails and fireroads, all of which can be used by bikers. In addition, there are various agencies at state level that also manage public land. Federal information centres can supply more details.

The best information source on local mountain-bike trails are bike shops and clubs. They usually have maps, too. County highway department maps show all the roads in a county. Details include whether the surface is paved or not. Older highways maps may show roads not shown on the newer ones. Abandoned settlements that appear on old maps must have had some means of getting there, so go and check it out.

Prohibitions

The 1964 Wilderness Act is a powerful piece of legislation that prevents any mechanical device from being used in a designated wilderness area. Mountain bikes fall within that definition. As there are more than 40 million hectares (100 million acres) of wilderness land, this reduces the amount of land open to mountain bikes and has led to conflict. These differences are in the process of being reconciled between mountain-bike users and conservation groups.

Even so, the International Mountain Bicycling Association, which represents American mountain-bike interests, is not in favour of changing the Wilderness Act to let mountain bikes in. The fear is that any changes would set a precedent that the powerful mining and logging lobbies could use as a means to get a foothold in these protected and environmentally sensitive areas.

The Rails to Trails Conservancy.

Over 7,000 miles (11,200 km) of disused railway track, forming over 650 trails, are open to bikers in America. The flat surfaces of these tracks make them good for covering long distances quickly. Not only do trails appear in towns and cities, they also pass through places that bikers would otherwise have difficulty getting to.

One of the finest examples is the Ironhorse Trail State Park in Washington State, a 110-mile (176-km) trail that passes through a 2½ mile (4-km) long tunnel and crosses trestle bridges that rise 200ft (60m) above the valley floors. Regional guides are available with details of this and other trails, including maps.

Long-distance trails

An ambitious project, aimed at creating a 3,000-mile (4,800-km) trail from Canada to Mexico, is being co-ordinated by the Adventure Cycling Association. Once completed, the Continental Divide Trail will be the longest in the world. It is estimated that when complete only 5 per cent will be on surfaced roads.

The America Discovery trail runs between California and Maryland and is the result of work by American hikers. Some 93 per cent will be open to bikers, with alternative routes being formed to accommodate them on the remaining 7 per cent.

24 hours of Canaan

Regarded as one of the toughest mountain-bike races in America, this 24-hour race is run on a 10-mile (16-km) single-track circuit. The event has grown from an entry of 36 teams in 1992 to 220 in 1994 – so if you're in West Virginia in the summer with nothing else to do, why not have a go!

Adventure Cycling Association

150 E Pine Street,
PO Box 8308,
Missoula,
Montana,
USA.

This organisation promotes the use of bicycles as a means of exploration, discovery and adventure, and can supply information on mountain-biking opportunities all over America.

International Mountain Bike Association (IMBA)

PO Box 3412043,
Los Angeles,
CA 90041,
USA.

This organization acts to promote mountain biking opportunities through environmentally and socially responsible use of the land. It is a good source of general information.

National Off Road Association (NORBA)

1750 East Boulder Street,
Colorado Springs,
Colorado 80707,
USA.

The governing body for mountain-bike racing in America.

The Rails to Trails Conservancy

1400 16th Street NW,
Suite 300,
Washington DC,
USA.

Promotes the recreational use of disused railway track and produces regional maps and guides.

Britain's North Yorkshire Moors offer great challenges and rewards to the adventurous cyclist.

EXPEDITION PLANNING

Taking your mountain bike on an expedition requires a great deal more preparation than going on a weekend jaunt, especially if you are planning to go abroad. This section acts as a checklist of points that you will need to think about when planning a longer ride. It covers the essentials of food, tools, clothing, shelter and transport, as well as matters such as health and insurance, and the best steps to take if things go wrong.

Planning a Ride

Before you dash off into the hills and out of sight, just take a bit of time to consider what you may need along the trail. It may take some time to get the right balance between carrying a complete repair kit and taking just the minimum you will need. Of course, you are always bound to leave behind precisely the tool you need. When your chain splits, and you are miles away from a connecting link or chain tool, the long walk home will give you plenty of time for reflection.

A basic kit for a normal day out can be packed into a light backpack, a bumbag or a handlebar bag. The essentials are a spare inner tube, a pump, and a puncture-repair kit.

Take on all rides

Whenever you go out on your bike, you should always wear your helmet; there can never be an excuse for not taking it. Carrying a spare innertube, pump and puncture-repair kit always makes sense. A basic first-aid kit tucked away is a sensible precaution in case you suffer one of those painful little tumbles.

Even on the sunniest day, it is a good idea to take at least a windproof top. Use one to fend off showers and to stop you getting chilled by the wind. They take up little space and don't weigh much.

Take on longer rides

For any ride off the road you must prepare for the unexpected. Some bits will come loose and others will break. Learn how to use your tools in comfort, light and warmth rather than waiting to learn how they work with cold fingers in driving rain in the dark.

You don't want to carry the weight of a full-blown workshop, so go around your bike and think through what the vulnerable areas might be and how you would fix or adjust them (see box on page 120). You will probably find that a chain tool, screwdriver, small adjustable spanner and several Allen keys will suffice for most eventualities. A rag for cleaning off dirt and oil can be used to wrap the tools in. Use plastic bags to hold small objects, such as Allen keys and chain-connecting pins.

You will see some neat-looking tool kits in your local bike shop, but check how practical they will be to use out on the trail before you part with your money. Tools with interchangeable parts may look a good idea but the bits are easy to lose; these kits often feature a wider range of tool sizes than you need on your bike.

All kitted out for a weekend expedition; note the hip belts that stop the rucksacks from sliding around.

Shimano-chain owners should make sure they take a spare connecting pin. Taya connecting links are a good idea for emergency use, but you will still need a chain tool to prepare the chain before it can be used.

Brake and gear cables don't take up much weight or space. Tape the cables in a coil, making sure the end doesn't stick out and cause an injury or get damaged. Keep them in a plastic bag together with some end-caps.

In the unlikely event that a spoke breaks you'll be glad you brought these along. Tape three or four together and fix them inside your seatpost. Take twice as many spoke nipples and make sure your spoke key fits them.

If three or four of you are travelling together, it can be a good idea to carry a Kevlar-beaded folding tyre. They take up a bit of room, but the load can be shared around.

Take some degreaser and plenty of lubricant, and make sure you use it. Remember to lubricate all the moving parts of your bike several times a day.

Take along sufficient spare nuts and bolts to be sure that you can replace any that work loose and get lost – for example, the little ones that fit carriers and bottle cages to the frame. Strong adhesive tape is also extremely useful for all manner of functions, from mending ripped tents to taping your carrier back together.

As well as a first-aid kit, you should also take a whistle and – depending on the terrain you expect to encounter – consider taking a survival bag (not just for you, but for anyone you come across who may need it). Finally you will need your maps, a compass and a source of energy – such as water with carbohydrate added – and some food.

A bumbag is useful for carrying tools, money and keys, and even for squeezing a windproof into. If it is cold and wet and you're taking food, you may want more room – perhaps a small rucksack, a bar bag or panniers.

Take on overnight rides

If you are planning a touring trip you will need to think about where you will be spending the nights. Camping equipment will add considerably to the weight and bulk of the bike, and it is far more enjoyable to plan a tour with hostel or bed-and-breakfast accommodation along the route – in which case, you will probably need to book well in advance, depending on the time of year.

When you are deciding what to pack, practise the old adage: put everything you plan to take in a heap and then throw half of it out.

More seriously, you should always ask yourself whether you will really need all of the things you would like to take.

Vulnerable parts

Bits of the bike that are most likely to need adjustment or repair are indicated in the following checklist. Always check your bike over thoroughly before you set out on a ride, so as to pre-empt these problems. Take sufficient tools with you to ensure that you can repair any of the following whilst on the trail:

- Handlebar fixings, especially bar ends
- Brakes, especially the locknuts
- Seat and post
- Chainrings
- Cages and carriers
- Gears, especially the jockey wheel
- Adjusters, hangers and derailleur adjusters
- Chain

If you find you cannot change gear, for any reason, using the derailleur adjuster screws should enable you to lock the derailleur into a get-you-home gear.

Accommodation

Youth hostel accommodation is ideal for cyclists, offering a bed and a choice of self-catering or canteen meals, plus, laundry and washing facilities.

For the odd night out in warm, dry weather a bivvy bag could be used, but a tent is far more practical. Sloping ridge tents are the smallest and lightest available, and two people can fit in at a squeeze, though they are too small to sit up in. Weighing less than 5 lbs (2.5 kg), a tent of this type is an essential for mountain-bike touring.

Sleeping bags

Sleeping bags should be chosen for low weight and bulk, though this will inevitably make them more expensive. The two fillings suitable for camping are down and artificial hollow-fibre materials.

Down weighs less, is less bulky and retains more warmth than hollow fibre, but is more expensive. Hollow fibre performs better when damp or wet. Bags come with different levels of filling, according to how much heat they retain. This warmth is measured by a season rating, but these ratings are not governed by any independent body and there is no consistent standard. Some manufacturers assume that you will be sleeping on a mat when they give a season rating.

Shop around and compare features before you buy, and ask other cyclists which bags they use or would recommend. Choose a bag that will keep you comfortable at the coldest temperatures you are likely to encounter, and no more. A bag that is too warm will cost you more money, take up more room and weigh more.

How warm?

How warm you feel in a bag will depend on several factors, not just on the ambient temperature. For example, your sensitivity to cold is affected by your overall health and fitness level, what you ate before going to bed and how hard you worked during the day. Wind, humidity and altitude also affect the degree to which cold is felt, as does the presence or absence of insulation under the bag.

To increase your warmth, try wearing a hat or using a liner. Fleece liners can be used to improve the warmth and insulation of a bag but they are bulky. Always sleep in clean dry clothes because salt from sweaty clothes will retain moisture.

Apart from the quality of the filling, the pattern and construction of the baffles that keep the filling in place affects the warmth of a bag. The greater the number of baffles, the more evenly spread the filling is over the body, rather than leaving cold spots.

Shell fabrics are a good idea because they allow the bag to drape around the body, and keep more of the insulation materials in contact with the body, rather than leaving large air pockets inside the bag. Both the lining and the shell fabric should let moisture through, however, to prevent water build up which will lower a bag's performance. Hoods, drawcords, zip baffles and tapered leg sections will all increase the warmth of a bag.

Season ratings

The following are the commonest season ratings you are likely to come across when shopping for a sleeping bag.

- Extreme. Such a bag is not necessary unless you are going up Everest.
- Alpine. It is unlikely that you will want to sleep outside if it is this cold. Consider using this type of bag for high-altitude camping.
- Four season. A winter bag for extreme cold.
- Three season. A winter or autumn bag.

Cooking and food

Do not carry food around with you if you can easily buy it en-route. Carbohydrate drink powder is not easy to find, however, so you will probably need to carry your own supplies. Plan to buy ready-cooked food or salads, rather than weighing yourself down with a mobile kitchen. If your budget allows, you can use cafes and restaurants on the way, or you can choose accommodation, such as youth hostels, that provide cooking facilities.

If you are going to more remote regions, and therefore have no choice but to cook along the way, choose your equipment carefully. Apart from weight and bulk, think about how practical it is to use.

Stoves

A stove must be stable and not likely to tip over with a heavy pan of boiling water on it. Never cook inside the tent. Take care once you have turned the stove off: it will still be very hot for some time to come and could easily burn you, your tent and anything else placed against it. Always take both matches and a cigarette lighter to light stoves with, even if your stove is self-igniting. Things always go wrong and you may well need a back up. Always fill your stove before using it, and not while it is hot or alight. If you refill a hot stove you risk fumes or spilt fuel vapourizing and igniting spontaneously.

Pans and cutlery

Choose materials that are easy to handle when hot – pans can then double as eating utensils, to save carrying plates. Aluminium pans are lighter than steel, though they have been suspected of contributing to Alzheimer's disease.

Aluminium pans are available with stainless steel linings. Make sure that pans will fit inside each other and thus take up as little room as possible.

Choose cutlery for lightness. Some people only take a knife for cutting, and eat with their fingers. Others just use a single wooden spoon with a shortened handle, though this might be a bit too minimalistic for some.

What to eat

After a hard day in the saddle you need to load up with carbohydrates. Pasta is one of the best forms and it is fairly light. Sauce can be made from powdered soup. This may not be a

Stove comparison		
Stove type	**For**	**Against**
Fuel blocks Military-style disposable packs that burn in a metal hearth which supports pans. Useful for the odd night or an emergency.	Cheap. Small and easy to light.	Flimsy, and difficult to control.
Meths A simple stove that is often supplied together with a pan set.	Easy to use, cheap and the fuel is widely available.	Slow cooking.
Petrol and multi-fuel (primus stoves) Most petrol stoves use other fuels too (eg paraffin) but check the instructions – certain petrol additives can clog the burner.	Quick cooking and the fuel is widely available.	Temperamental to light. The fuel jets clog with dirty fuel or the wrong type of fuel.
Gas The cannister attaches to the burner directly, to form the base of the cooker, or separately via a tube.	Easy to light and quick cooking.	Gas cannisters are not available everywhere.

Heavily laden panniers affect the bike's handling characteristics, so spread loads evenly.

gourmet diet, but you will survive for a few days before it gets to you. Semolina is also easy to cook and carry.

Dried foods that only need water adding are not to everybody's taste, and the packs need to be checked to make sure that they provide sufficient energy. They can be made more palatable with curry or some other flavouring, so try putting some of your favourite spices together in a polythene bag or container.

Water

Drinking water can sometimes be difficult to find, so it is sensible to carry sterilising tablets for purifying water from rivers or streams. This will not remove the danger from heavy-metal contamination or pesticides, so be careful in your choice of water source.

Panniers, carriers and rucksacks

When you start to load up your bike, remember that the handling characteristics will change as the centre of gravity is shifted. This may dictate what you use for carrying your luggage, and where you pack it on the bike.

Panniers may seem the obvious solution, but they do have disadvantages. They make the bike more difficult to carry when you have to lift it over obstructions. They also have a tendency to catch on undergrowth, and can easily tip you off the bike if this happens when you are travelling at speed.

A rucksack gives you more control over the bike's handling but it does limit the amount that you can carry. It is also more tiring on the back and arms, and it can get uncomfortable when the weather is hot.

You certainly shouldn't consider carrying more then 20 lbs (9 kg) on your back. If the rucksack weighs more, start looking at other

Properly kitted out for the trail and sensibly loaded you can enjoy your biking expeditions to the full.

places to carry the weight. Choose a sack with a hip belt that will stop the bag sliding from side to side. Take care that the belt and buckle are properly adjusted so that they do not dig into your stomach when you are riding.

Don't get too big a bag, or one with protruding side pockets, because this will obscure your vision when you want to see behind, which you will need to do in traffic.

Some rackpacks and panniers convert to a rucksack which offers more flexibility. Whatever you choose, line the insides with plastic bags for extra waterproofing.

Tools

Apart from the tools you would normally carry, think about what you would need if you had to undertake major repairs. Spare parts, such as cables and bearings, can be purchased as you go, but you do not want to have to buy new and expensive tools, so take tools to fit all the bikes in your party and take an adjustable spanner big enough to cope with all nuts, including the headset.

Sun protection

Wearing eye protection, with clear or dark lenses, is advisable, and not just against bright sun and harmful ultraviolet rays. Stones, mud and insects can all get in your eyes.

Sunblock is essential, and not just for hot days. Even in a cooling breeze, it is easy to get burnt – and don't forget the back of the neck, which is very vulnerable.

Clothes

You may get away with wearing one set of clothes for several days, so long as you don't get wet – but don't count on it. A good waterproof top with a hood should keep your torso dry through most things, but legs are a different matter. Even with Goretex socks or boots and waterproof leggings the chances are that

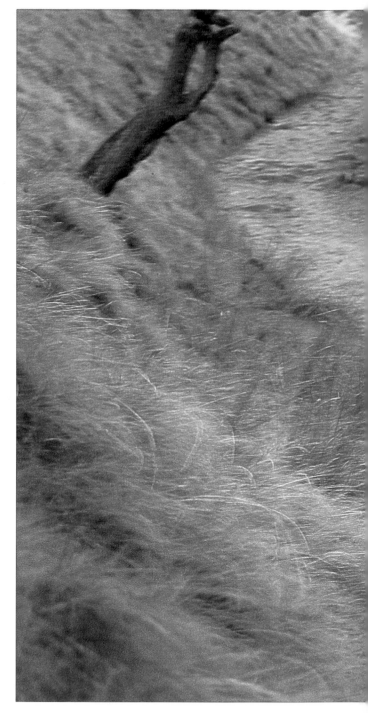

your feet will get wet. Even for a short trip, you should take at least one change of clothing and make sure you are completely dry before changing into it, otherwise the benefits of swapping your clothes will all be lost.

When you are going away for several days, you'll have to think about how many changes of clothes you will need for the duration, and how you are going to get them clean and dry. Obviously, life is easier if you choose clothing treated against odours that is easy to wash and dry. Only take as much concentrated washing powder or liquid as you will need. Another option is to post your clothes home once you've finished wearing them.

Travelling abroad

Proper preparation for an extended trip should start long before you leave home. Some of the points mentioned in this chapter may seem rather obvious, but it is precisely because they are so obvious that people very often forget them or leave them until it is too late.

Passport and visas

Check that your passport has at least six months to run (twelve months would be even better). Some countries will not let you in if your passport is due to expire. Remember that it can take several weeks to have your passport renewed, especially around busy holiday periods.

The visa requirements of countries vary from time to time and will be different from one nationality to another. Check with the appropriate embassy, and make sure you tell them what nationality passport you hold.

The ease and speed with which visas are dispensed varies greatly. Allow plenty of time. Some applications need supporting with all kinds of information and documentation. If you plan to travel to more than one country, obtain all necessary visas before you leave home. Trying to get them outside your native country is not always possible, and it is a lot less hassle at home.

On arrival, you may be asked to show your return or onward ticket and give proof that you have sufficient funds to support yourself. The sheer fact of having a visa is therefore no guarantee of entry. Of course, if you are carrying travellers' cheques, and have a return ticket, there should not be a problem.

Air travel

The days when airline tickets were sold through shady backstreet bucketshops may have gone, but the business of buying airline tickets is still shrouded in mystique and uncertainty. The surest and safest way is to buy at full price direct from the airline, but this is also by far the most expensive. Buying from other sources, you need to be aware of any limitations to the way the ticket can be used. With most cheap tickets, it is not possible to change your flight once booked, and the ticket could be inflexible in other ways, such as the timing of your return journey.

If you are travelling for three months or more, you may want a bit more flexibility in your flying arrangements, and buying the cheapest ticket may not always be the best option. Given the safety record of some national airlines, you may also prefer to pay more to fly with a more responsible carrier.

Flying with a bike

As well as concern for your own safety, you need to choose an airline that will look after your bike. Most airlines will, so long as you take a few precautions and pack it sensibly. A cycle bag is the best option, but it leaves you with a problem at the other end – what to do with the bag while you are on tour. You could try posting it to yourself *poste-restante* to the local post office, but you need to be sure that there is not a time limit on the collection of *poste-restante* mail. Train stations in some countries have long-term baggage storage facilities. Alternatively, you could dispense with the bag and wrap the bike in dispensable cardboard held together with tape.

Whatever method you use, you will need to remove the wheels, the seat post and the pedals. Once the wheels are removed, it is a good idea to bolt some spindles to the front and rear forks. This will help prevent damage to the frame while the bike is in the hands of airport staff. The handlebars should be turned and tied, or taped, to the top tube to prevent movement. Deflate your tyres, and the air suspension system, if you have one.

Removing the derailleur is a sensible precaution, because it can easily be knocked and damaged. You may be able to wrap it up and tape it to the frame to avoid having to remove the cable.

Rail travel

Although a lot of what has been said about air travel could be applied to trains as well, there is not usually the same degree of concern. In any case you will probably use the train more frequently, and won't want to go to the same bother every time you travel. You are far more likely to want to be able to ride the bike in and out of the station.

Load the bike yourself if you are allowed. For even greater confidence, you should travel with the bike. Usually the bike will have to be carried in a separate compartment or van, but you may be allowed to stay with it. Expect to pay for the service.

Money

Carrying large sums of money around is a constant worry, as you are always wary of being mugged or losing your money. There are several things you can do to avoid this. Don't keep all your money together. Instead, use a purse or wallet to keep small amounts and put the rest in a secure place where it cannot be seen, preferably on your person, and not on your bike, which is, itself, liable to being stolen. Use low-denomination travellers' cheques and notes so that, if your purse or wallet is stolen, you do not lose large quantities of money in one go.

Credit cards are a useful back-up, but be careful. Fraudulent use of your card may not come to light until you get your next statement, and long after you are home. Keep the carbon papers and destroy them yourself, and try to avoid leaving open credit card vouchers if at all possible. Sometimes this is unavoidable, if you are hiring a car or booking into a hotel, because you will be asked to leave a signed but open voucher as a deposit. If this happens, be sure to get a copy of the completed voucher before you leave the hotel, or when you return the car.

Before you leave home, you might consider making arrangements with your bank to have money transferred to you at regular intervals. Don't expect this to be a same-day service, however; you may find yourself going backwards and forwards to the receiving bank for several days until the money comes through.

Many countries still have currency controls. You will have to produce your passport when you change money, and you will receive money-exchange forms as a record of the transaction. These must be kept until you have left the country, and they must be produced if you wish to change your money back.

Some currencies can only be exchanged in the country of origin. Black markets operate in these countries, offering higher than official rates, but so do conmen and paid informers.

Maps and guides

On your first visit to a country, especially an undeveloped one, a guide book is essential. The guide books published by Lonely Planet are among the best for budget travellers. Don't rely on them totally, however, as such things as telephone numbers and opening times do change and occasionally they get things wrong.

Maps vary widely from country to country. The biggest problem a mountain biker faces is knowing whether a path or track is passable on a bike. The scale on some maps does not allow every track to be shown in detail, so buy one at a large enough scale for your needs. You will need to know how to read the features on a map.

Stanfords of London has a comprehensive stock of maps and guides from around the world. They offer a mail-order service (Stanfords, 12–14 Long Acre, London WC2E 9LP, United Kingdom. Tel: +44 171 836 1321; fax: +44 171 836 0189).

Back-up

On a long-haul trip of several weeks duration, the need for spares and replacements increases. In a developed country replacements should be easy to obtain locally, but where the infrastructure does not cater for mountain bikes, another method of getting spares is needed.

Tyres, chains, sprockets and chainrings are not items you want to carry with you, though your drivetrain will almost certainly need replacing after 1,000 miles (1,600 km) of off-road cycling. Rather than wait for a failure to happen, it is best to change the chain, even if there is still some wear left.

If you (or someone else) can send spares to places along your route (using *poste-restante* services) they will be waiting for you when you arrive. By operating a policy of replacement at these supply points, you can cut down on the worry of searching for spares. Alternatively, contact your national cycling touring club for local contacts.

If you are depending on someone else to send you spares, make sure that they have full details of your bike – especially the seat-post diameter and bottom-bracket width; if an emergency does arise, the possibility of being sent the wrong bit is thus reduced.

If the worst should happen, and your frame gets damaged, frame builders can be thin on the ground in some parts of the world. Try a local workshop – in my experience, the noisier and busier the better.

Fitting in

Your explorations in unknown lands may leave the folks back home in awe , but the people you meet along the route may not share your sense that you are a brave pioneer. People live and spend their lives in places that seem novel and unusual to you, so try not to cause offence by your attitude or behaviour.

Keep any views you may have about their religion, politicians or rulers to yourself. Respect local customs and habits, especially when it comes to dress, nudity and alcohol. This is not just a case of upsetting the locals – there is a real danger that you may commit a criminal offence.

The largest barrier you are likely to encounter is language. Make the effort to learn simple phrases. With languages where the script is unfamiliar (Chinese or Arabic, for example) it is a good idea to get someone to write down the address of where you want to go in the local language.

(RIGHT) All the hassle of organizing a cycling holiday is worth it once you get out on the trail.

If Things go Wrong

All your planning should include knowing how to react to catastrophe. In your mind, you should be able to recognize when it is dangerous to carry on. Some people wrongly confuse this with not having the willpower to carry on. The two are totally separate issues.

Common sense tells us that we should always let someone who cares about what happens to us know where we are going and when we will be back. Leave details of your itinerary with a friend or family member; in the absence of that, inform the hotelier, hostel warden or even the rescue services (in the case of dangerous terrain) where you are going and when you expect to return.

Damaged bikes

When things go wrong it always happens miles from anywhere, in cold rain and fading light. If it is a bike problem and you are on your own, it could be that you are simply going to have to bite the bullet and walk. If you are with someone, then try looping your spare tubes together to form a towrope and pull the damaged bike and rider (having removed the bike chain, if necessary).

A badly bent wheel isn't going to suffer any more damage, so don't be afraid of using brute force to get it rolling again.

Personal injury

The real problems start when somebody is too badly injured to continue. If you are on your own, use your whistle to summon help. The recognized international distress signal is a sequence of six long blasts, repeated at one-minute intervals (or six flashes on a torch). To reply to a distress call, use three flashes or blasts.

If there are two of you, and one of you decides to fetch help, leave the victim with as much warm clothing as you can spare without putting yourself in danger. Before you leave, make sure you know the precise location of your injured partner. It wouldn't be the first time that the rescuer couldn't find his way back to the victim or tell anyone where he was.

A good knowledge of first aid will give you a lot of confidence to deal with an injured person, so go on a first-aid course (or on a refresher course if your memory of the correct procedures is growing thin).

Trouble abroad

Disasters abroad are the most worrying. Don't expect the local embassy to come running to your assistance; they won't. They are there to represent political and business interests, and they show little concern for their fellow citizens unless they are in a life-threatening situation, such as war, terrorism, civil disturbance or a natural disaster. If this happens, make it your priority to get out and don't worry about your bike.

Fortunately such incidents are rare. You are more likely to fall ill or get knocked over by the traffic. If you become sick or get injured away from home let someone know where you are and the extent of your problems. You don't want to alarm them, but it makes a lot of difference if people are aware of your predicament, especially if things get worse.

Insurance

Apart from the normal worries of health when travelling in a foreign country, mountain bikers run the added risk of injury.

The way to relieve this worry is to obtain insurance before you leave home. Make sure it covers you not only against theft, damage and

Mishaps are an inevitable feature of life on the trail, so keep your first-aid knowledge up to date.

other travel mishaps, but (most importantly) that it will cover medical costs and repatriation if that becomes necessary. Tailor-made travel and medical insurance for cyclists is often available through the national body for cyclists in your home country (see pages 102 to 114). Whichever policy you choose, be sure to check that mountain biking is not defined as a dangerous sport that is not covered by your insurance cover.

Reciprocal health agreements often exist between nations. European Union residents are entitled to receive treatment from other EU countries, but you must obtain all the relevant documentation before your trip (this is usually available from post offices). Some countries belonging to the Commonwealth also have informal reciprocal arrangements.

Consult your doctor regarding inoculations well in advance of your trip. You may need a course of injections that start up to three months before you leave. Malaria prevention, for example, always starts before you leave; how long before depends on the type of medication prescribed. Bear in mind that there have been some major changes in medical thinking on the prevention of malaria, cholera and hepatitis A and B. Press your doctor to make sure you are being given the latest information, and, if in doubt, double check with a reliable source, such as a tropical diseases clinic.

Concerns over healthcare standards have led many travellers to take their own supplies of needles, syringes and medically prescribed drugs. If you plan to do this, make sure that the drugs you need do not break that country's laws. Often it helps to obtain a letter from your doctor explaining what the drugs are and certifying that they are medically necessary.

Your first-aid kit should be well thought-out, and this is something your doctor may be able to give some advice on. Make sure that sterile items are stored carefully, because they don't stand up to the rigours of travel very well, and the packaging can easily split.

A trip to the dentist before setting off for foreign fields may not seem the most obvious of preparation priorities but it is worth considering if you plan to be away for several weeks and you haven't had a check-up recently.

Tummy troubles and minor injuries

Diarrhoea is an unpleasant experience at any time. If you are a cyclist, needing high amounts of food and a properly functioning metabolism, this interruption to the system is serious. Apart from loss of food, more dangerous still is the dehydration that occurs. Don't let the situation get to the point where you can no longer carry on. Stop and rest for as long as it takes to recover. If you have any choice in the matter, choose somewhere with good food and clean water for your recuperation.

Picking up a tummy bug is all too easy. Water is an obvious source, so buy bottled water and make sure that the top is sealed. If this is not available, treat the water with purifying tablets. Don't trust anybody else with this task. Boiling water for three minutes will kill most things, but lower air pressure at high altitude means that water boils at a lower temperature, and so is not as effective.

Carbonated drinks may not always be safe. Often these are just flavoured fizzy tap water. Do not use ice or eat salads unless you can be absolutely confident that purified water has been used. Don't eat fruit unless peeled by yourself. Only eat freshly cooked food. Choose foods that require cooking at high temperatures (deep-fried, for example) and that are served straight away.

Cuts and bruises are all part of mountain biking. In some climates, especially where the humidity is high or where you are always wet, minor injuries can become infected before they heal. Insect bites, particularly from mosquitoes, can also become inflamed and infected. Problems like this are compounded if the injury is to a foot or some other part of the body that is constantly being rubbed, wetted or dirtied. If you have a persistent problem seek medical attention. Don't wait until the injury is inflamed and causing discomfort.

First-aid

Problem	Action
Cuts and grazes	Prevent infection by covering the wound with a bandage until it can be thoroughly cleaned under running water.
Snake bites	Puncture marks in the skin and severe pain at the site of the bite are indications of a serious problem. Arrange urgent hospital treatment. Do *not* try to suck out the venom, cut the wound with a knife or apply a tourniquet.
Shock	Symptoms are pale clammy skin, nausea and shallow breathing. Lay the patient on his/her back, with the legs slightly raised. Cover with coats or a blanket. Reassure the patient and stay with him/her while someone else goes to phone for an ambulance. Do *not* let the casualty move unnecessarily, smoke, drink or eat.
Hypothermia	Apathy, confusion, shivering and marble-like skin are all symptoms of hypothermia caused by prolonged exposure to cold, wet or windy conditions. Shelter the patient from wind or rain and lay him/her on a dry surface. Remove wet clothes, and insulate the patient with any available dry clothing or sleeping bags. You can also use polythene bags or newspapers. Cover the head. Send for help but never leave the patient alone. Give a hot drink if possible.
Heat exhaustion	Symptoms are headaches, dizziness, excessive sweating, nausea, muscle cramps and rapid breathing. Move the patient to cool shaded surroundings. Lay him/her on the ground. Raise and support the patient's legs to improve blood flow to the brain. Give the patient as much cool weak salt solution (1 teaspoon per pint of water) as he/she can drink.

SERVICE CHARTS

Mountain bikes come in for a lot of rough treatment – far more so than road bikes. This makes it even more essential that the bike is serviced regularly. Use this section as a checklist for the various vulnerable parts of your bike. The Servicing Schedule tells you what to do to keep your bike in peak condition, and how often. The Fault Finder covers the most common problems and tells you how to sort them out.

Servicing schedule

Job	Frequency	What to do
Cleaning.	After every ride.	Clean all dirt and mud off the bike. Clean and lubricate the drive chain.
Gear adjustment (see page 32).	Every 1–4 weeks. Don't let the gear change become imprecise. Cleaning off dirt and grass will often improve the gear change, but fine tune the adjustment regularly.	Use barrel adjuster to fine tune the gear change. Adjust the jockey wheel position. Check the travel of the derailleur.
Brake adjustment (see page 40).	As braking becomes less effective and more brake movement is required.	Adjust barrel adjuster. If blocks are worn down, replace them.
Chain replacement (see page 36).	When chain has stretched $\frac{1}{16}$ inch over 12 links, and before it has stretched $\frac{1}{8}$ inch over 12 links. Check monthly.	Replace chain. Check whether the sprockets need changing too.
Sprocket replacement (see page 28).	When the new chain jumps over the teeth on the sprocket. Consider replacing this every time a new chain is fitted to ensure an even wear rate.	Use chain whip and lockring tool to replace the sprocket. Check freehub wear.
Wheel bearings (see page 28).	After heavy water contamination. If wheel axles become submerged in water, strip down as soon as possible. Otherwise wheel bearings should be serviced every 3–6 months.	Strip down wheel hub. Replace all bearings and pitted cones. Clean and pack in waterproof grease. If hubs are worn and in need of replacement, consider a wheel upgrade.

Job	Frequency	What to do
Wheel truing (see page 23).	Check after every ride for small variations. Every 1–3 months remove tyre and check condition of spokes and lubricate nipples.	Remove tyre and mark high, low and side imperfections. Use spoke key to adjust.
Bottom bracket (see page 38).	Cup-and-cone bottom brackets need servicing whenever they become submerged in water, or after 3–6 months, depending on use. If any play can be felt in the bottom bracket service immediately.	Remove pedal crank. Dismantle and service cup-and-cone bottom bracket. Consider upgrading to a sealed cassette bottom bracket.
Headset/Aheadset (see page 46).	If you can feel knocking coming from the front forks check headset. If it is loose then service. Strip down every 3–6 months.	Strip down headset and replace bearings, clean and regrease assembly. If headset is worn then replace. Consider having headtube faced to ensure correct fit for new headset.
Cables (see page 42).	Clean after every ride. Strip down every 3–6 months. Replace every 6–12 months or if the action gets stiff.	Don't let muck and oil accumulate on the cables. When stripped down lightly oil and wipe off. Use penetrating fluid to flush out inners until clean. Always fit end caps

Note: Frequency of servicing depends very much on how often you ride your bike and the conditions it is ridden in. This schedule is for guidance only and relates to a bike that is ridden once or twice a week on a regular basis. It is important to recognize that water is your enemy because rust will damage your bearings whether you are riding your bike or not. Water has a habit of finding its way into your bike in all manner of ways so don't underestimate it. It is equally important to recognize when wear is manifesting itself so that you don't increase wear rates on associated components. This is especially important with regard to the chain and drivetrain.

Fault finder

Fault	Cause	Cure
Chain jumps over sprockets or chain ring.	Worn chain.	Change chain (see page 36). If the problem persists, change the sprockets and chain rings (see page 28).
Chain shifts out of sprocket.	Derailleur-stop screws not adjusted properly.	Adjust derailleur stop screws (see page 34).
Poor or inaccurate gear shift.	Indexing out of adjustment or cable fouled with dirt. In muddy conditions, clogged chain, sprockets and jockey wheels.	Clean and lubricate cable and mechanism (see page 43). If the problem persists, adjust the indexing (see page 34). If you still have a problem check that the hanger is not damaged.
Poor braking.	Rims wet.	Apply brakes until dry.
	Blocks too far from rim, or too much travel in brake lever.	Adjust brakes (see page 40).
	Brakes fading.	Fit brake pads made of harder compounds (see page 39).
Brakes squeal.	Poor toe-in.	Set toe-in correctly (see page 41).
Clicking pedal.	Excess play in bearing.	Service or repair pedal (see pages 49 and 51).
Wheels, bottom bracket, headset or pedals stiff or don't turn freely.	Bearings too tight or contaminated with water.	Service and ensure correct adjustment (see pages 28, 38, 46 and 49).

Fault	Cause	Cure
Creaking from around bottom bracket.	Chainrings loose.	Tighten chainrings (see page 32).
	Pedal crank and bottom bracket axle need attention.	Remove pedal cranks, clean and apply grease sparingly to the axle surface where it is in contact with crank, and wipe off excess (see pages 49 and 51).
	Bottom bracket needs attention.	Check for wear or damage, and service or repair as required (see page 38).
	Crack in frame, possibly from impact.	Inspect frame for cracks. If none are obvious, remove bottom bracket and check inside for small cracks. Get frame builder to repair.
Wheels, bottom bracket, headset or pedals have a lot of play and, although they turn freely, don't spin very well	Bearings too loose or worn.	Service and ensure proper adjustment (see pages 28, 38, 46 and 49).
Clunking from front forks.	Headset loose or worn.	Adjust headset and consider servicing (see page 46).
Brake blocks rub against wheel rim.	Brakes not aligned properly.	Set brakes up (see page 40).
	Wheel out of true.	Adjust spoke tension to make wheel round and even (see page 23).

Acknowledgements

All the photographs in this book were taken and supplied by Tim Woodcock except for the following:

p8-9; STOCKFILE: Chris Patient
p10-11; Simon Blacker
p69; STOCKFILE: Steve Behr
p102-3; STOCKFILE: Chris Patient
p104; STOCKFILE: Mark Gallop
p106-7; STOCKFILE: Rory Hitchins
p110-11; STOCKFILE: Steve Behr.

Additional illustrations: Jon Eland.
Research assistance: Howard Turner.

Manufacturers who helped with the project are: E Reece *(Univega Alpina MTB)*, M Adison *(Park Tools, Finish Line cycle-care products, VistaLite lights, Profile bar-ends, Blackburn mini-pump)*, Karrimor Cycle Equipment *(Giro helmets, Avocet computers, Karrimor cycle clothing, panniers and rucsac)*, Cool Tool UK *(Trail Tools)*, Patrick Schils (UK) Ltd *(John Luck shoes)*, Fisher of Finchley Ltd *(Ritchey Logic SPD pedals)*, Sensible Products *(Crud Catcher and Crud Guard)* and Ison Distribution *(ID jockey wheels)*. Thanks also to Ralph Coleman Cycles, Taunton and Finch and Sons, Reigate, for supplying mountain-bike props at very short notice.

Index